250 AMAZING HUNTING TIPS

THE BEST TACTICS AND TECHNIQUES TO GET YOUR GAME THIS SEASON

DEER • BEAR • WATERFOWL • SMALL GAME AND MORE!

LAMAR UNDERWOOD
and
NATE MATTHEWS

Illustrations by John Rice

Skyhorse Publishing

Skyhorse Publishing books may be purchased in bulk at special discounts for sales promotion, corporate gifts, fund-raising, or educational purposes. Special editions can also be created to specifications. For details, contact the Special Sales Department, Skyhorse Publishing, 307 West 36th Street, 11th Floor, New York, NY 10018 or info@skyhorsepublishing.com.

Visit our website at www.skyhorsepublishing.com.

10 9 8 7 6 5 4 3 2 1

Library of Congress Cataloging-in-Publication Data

Underwood, Lamar.

250 amazing hunting tips : the best tactics and techniques to get your game this season : deer,. bear,. waterfowl,. small game,and more! / Lamar Underwood and Nate Matthews ; illustrations by John Rice.

pages cm

ISBN 978-1-63220-303-8 (pbk. : alk. paper) — ISBN 978-1-63220-950-4 (ebook) 1. Hunting—Handbooks, manuals, etc. I. Matthews, Nate. II. Title. III. Title: Two hundred and fifty amazing hunting tips.

SK33.U527 2015

639'.1—dc23

2015021854

Printed in the United States of America

250
AMAZING HUNTING TIPS

Contents

Introduction

The other evening, after I had spent the day going over material for this book, my wife made a remark that brought doubt and fear crashing into my thoughts like lightning bolts. She simply said, "The newspaper had a section today called '101 Grilling Tips.' I looked at them all and didn't find a single one to be useful."

Suddenly, I felt almost ill. I thought about picking up the phone and calling Nate Matthews, my co-editor and writer on this book. Was a fate similar to "101 Grilling Tips" in store for our book—multiplied two and a half times? Were our tips destined to be ignored, cast aside with shrugs and expressions of disappointment? It didn't seem possible, yet there it was: the possibility that we would not connect with our audience.

Instead of allowing my anguish to continue unabated, I decided to look at "101 Grilling Tips" myself. I only liked a couple of the tips. The others were bland, without any juice to make me want to whip the cover off the Weber. My confidence in the work Nate and I were finishing began to rise again. Later, over the next few days as I gave our tips a final reading, that confidence level peaked out again. Today, ready to commit our tips to print, I guarantee our readers that they are going to find many, many useful tips. And I shall go even further by saying that many of the tips are so important that they mean the difference between success and failure on your hunt.

Yes, a single tip on hunting can carry that kind of importance behind it. If followed, it can mean you're literally bringing home the bacon. Ignored or forgotten, it can mean you're coming home only with that tired old expression, "Sure was nice being in the woods today." Yea . . . sure . . . it was nice. There's no disputing that. But you have nothing new to put into the freezer.

Allow me, if you will, to try to press my point about tips home with an example.

My personal deer hunting education was slow in evolving. I'm an Army brat, who grew up mostly in the south where my hunting was focused on smoothbore opportunities. Using dogs to drive deer to standers was still in vogue back then and never appealed to me, especially with the great hunting we had for quail, doves, ducks, squirrels, and rabbits.

There came a long-awaited morning, however, when as a young man I became a serious player in the great game known as whitetail deer hunting. I was settled against the trunk of an enormous white oak in the heart of classic whitetail country among the folded hills and ridges of Pennsylvania. Under a flashlight's glow, with my friend Larry's direction, I had swept aside leaves and sticks to make my nest as quiet as possible. I had a pack with a thermos and sandwiches, and in my hands rested a Winchester lever-action .30-30 with iron sights. The rifle triggered memories of the Daisy Red Ryder I had grown up using. When I was all set, Larry moved away to work another part of the ridge.

At first light, the horizon was cut from steel—black lumps of white pines, the knife-like rim of a distant ridge looming above the forest. Without wind, the stillness seemed almost electric as I shivered in the cold, nervous to the raw edge at the thought of a buck coming my way.

When the crows began to patrol, their raucous cries announcing that it was time for things to get moving, I detected the rustle of squirrels in the branches overhead. As the light came on, I began to hear occasional gunshots, echoing from the distant ridge.

The gunfire made me nervous. For some time, I had been hearing about reckless deer hunters, shooting at anything that moved. "Oh, I had a couple of brush shots." That often-repeated comment wasn't funny to me.

Suddenly, the sound of a limb breaking jerked my attention toward the trees to my left. I strained to see. Nothing! The sound came again, louder still, and followed this time by the dry rustle of leaves beings shuffled. I could only think of one thing that could make that much noise in the deer woods: another hunter! I was suddenly very, very afraid. I stood up, waving and shouting, "Hi there!"

There was a moment of total silence. Then, in an explosion of crashing brush, the buck of my dreams bounced into the full light in a clearing between the pines, white tail flagging, then was instantly gone before I could even think of raising my rifle.

I stood there, stunned, hurt to the core. I was thinking terrible thoughts about myself. About being stupid, fumbling the ball, blowing my big chance. I was sure I would never have such an opportunity again.

I felt like heading for our car, going home. But I sat back down instead, trying to get a grip on myself. I had no faith that another chance would come my way, but I knew the game would not be over until sundown. I would play it out, give Lady Luck a chance to shine on me again.

Gradually, the forest worked its therapy on my beleaguered spirit. Bird activity was plentiful— crows, blue jays, chickadees, woodpeckers, juncos were on the move and calling. As always when I'm on a stand, they furnished a interesting sideshow during the hours of waiting for game to show. Then, about noontime, I noticed that the squirrels were moving as industriously as they had been at dawn. Strange, I thought, there must be some dirty weather around. I can't see it coming, but they can feel it coming.

I knew I was getting back into the groove then, focused on nature instead of myself. I dug into my pack for the sandwiches and coffee. They were very satisfying. I felt my confidence rising, and I realized now I owned something precious: the image of that buck in the clearing between the pines, the light full on what William Faulkner in a hunting tale called ". . . that rocking chair he carried."

I did not get my "rocking chair" buck that day. That night, it snowed, and two days later I shot a fork-horn buck. For the first time in my life—though certainly not the last—I found myself saying to the other fellows, "Well, boys, you can't eat horns."

As for the buck of my dreams . . . he would have to wait. And I could not help but think, rather bitterly: Why didn't Larry tell me: Bucks can make considerable noise when they're out for a morning stroll and haven't been disturbed. One single tip . . . that's all it would have taken. A tip I did not have.

If you've ever used the expression "I'd rather be lucky than good," then you just might be a whitetail deer hunter. You're a card-carrying dreamer out to beat the odds, your heart set on a rack for the wall and a freezer where packets of venison take up most of the room. You're not discouraged by the possibility that this may not be your year to bag a buck, for the pull of the deer woods and deer camp are strong. You've just got to be out there, watching the weather, checking for sign, enjoying the company of good buddies.

That the task of bagging a whitetail buck—any buck!—requires skills is obvious to the brethren of Hunter Orange. While they are animals of fairly rigid habit, whitetail deer are interesting and complex creatures prone to a witch's brew—for hunters anyway—of contradictory behavioral patterns that are sometimes hard to understand and impossible to predict. When you think you have a lock on where they're feeding, they move to some other dining halls in another part of the forest or croplands. The white oak patch where you scouted a buck feeding a week before turns out to be empty on opening day—except for its colony of squirrels. This list of failed game plans could go on and on.

You think you know what the deer will be doing. Perhaps you do. But all too often it seems like they're doing it somewhere else—somewhere you don't know about! And don't think for a minute that your quarry doesn't know you're coming.

Opening Day. The pre-dawn explodes with noise, like a bomb going off. A deer, especially a veteran "survivor" buck, would have to be deaf not to know what's going on. The cacophony includes the sounds of engines being revved up, wheels spinning in the mud, truck and SUV doors slamming, the snick-snick of gun actions being worked, and a myriad of shouts, "Hey, Joe, you goin' to the Oak Tree stand?" "I'll meet you at noon by the apple orchard." "Oh no, I forgot my shells!"

Well, perhaps we can get lucky. Happens all the time. Just drop by any check-in station, and you'll see people there who wouldn't know a scrape from a hog wallow. Nevertheless, they will have tags on bucks.

The goal Nate Matthews and I have set for ourselves is to give you something to cut the odds on your next hunt, for whatever game interests you—whitetail deer, mallards, pheasants, moose, you name it.

Nate and I come your way from a background of working with some of the most highly respected magazines in the outdoor field—*Field & Stream*, *Sports Afield*, and *Outdoor Life*. We do not present ourselves as experts in the various hunts we cover. But we know the people who are—and you will find them in the pages ahead.

If you feel lucky, I'm sure you will carry that on your next hunt. As I have suggested, Lady Luck makes a fine companion. Nate and I hope, however, that you will be taking some of these tips along to supplement the Lady's efforts. You might be on a deer stand at dawn and hear something shuffling your way, breaking sticks, making noise. Sounds like another hunter, except . . . oh yes . . . there was this tip you heard somewhere. About bucks sometimes making noise instead of sneaking in. You keep watching . . . and then raise your gun. Yes!

Sometimes, just the right tip is all you need to have a great day.

Good luck!

—Lamar Underwood

CHAPTER 1

White-tailed Deer Hunting

1. Don't Shoot Bucks That Look Insecure

When you first see a buck, take a moment to check its posture. Dominant bucks hold their heads high and walk loosely with their tails held straight out. A subordinate buck walks with stiff legs and a hunched back, and keeps its tail between its legs. If you see a good buck in a subordinate posture, consider holding your shot. It could mean there's a real monster in the area.

2. Find Small Bucks Near Big Scrapes

If you're looking to shoot a buck quickly during the rut and aren't much concerned about the size of its antlers, look for a large scrape that's torn up, irregularly shaped, and looks like it's being used by more than one deer. Younger, more submissive bucks frequent such scrapes. Since these bucks are less wary and more numerous than trophy animals, you'll stand a good chance of filling your tag faster than you would when hunting scrapes made by solitary (and often bigger) deer.

3. The Surefire Spot for Big Bucks

Don't give up on a hunting spot when you learn a big whitetail has been taken there. If it was a dominant buck, a host of suitors for this vacated territory will soon move in. The sudden void may dramatically increase other bucks' activity. If you can hunt where another hunter has already bagged a big buck, do it!

4. See More Deer by Scanning an Area Twice

Immediately after stopping at a vantage point, allow your eyes to relax and move them slowly back and forth over the surrounding terrain without focusing on any specific feature. Relaxed eyes automatically focus on any movement within their field of vision. If no deer are moving in your immediate vicinity, shift to a tightly focused analysis of every piece of cover you can see. Peer into the shadows, looking for pieces of deer—bits of antler, the curve of an ear, or the horizontal line of a back. Move to your next vantage point once you're satisfied that you've probed all the places a deer might be hiding.

5. Don't Use Too Much Freshly Collected Scent

If you plan to use scent collected from the glands of a freshly-killed deer, make sure to use less of it than you would of the bottled stuff. The fresh gland scent will be much more potent than what you can buy commercially.

6. Three Steps to Proper Still-hunting

Proper still-hunting can be described as a three-step process. Step one is to stand motionless behind an object that will break up your outline while searching the surrounding area thoroughly for any sign that deer are present. Step two is to remain still and use your eyes to pick out a way forward that lets you place your feet on the quietest ground cover possible, such as bare rock, moss, wet leaves, or soft snow. Step three is to scan the woods for deer one more time, then slowly and silently navigate the route you've picked out. Repeat steps one through three until you find your buck. Do not rush. A good still-hunter will sometimes take an hour to traverse 100 yards of heavy cover.

7. Catch Wary Peak-season Bucks Off Guard during Lunch

Because of increased pressure during the rut, mature bucks will often change their patterns to avoid hunter activity. Many will become nocturnal, but a significant number instead spend more time searching for does during the middle of the day, when most hunters are back at camp taking naps and eating lunch. Try sitting your stand during the hours before and after noon to catch these deer off guard.

8. Use Different Routes to Your Deer Stand at Sunrise and Sunset

Never walk through a crop field in the early morning when approaching a deer stand set up near its edge. Deer are likely

feeding in this field under cover of darkness—you will startle them if you don't take a back route to your stand. The opposite is true when you're approaching the same stand during the afternoon or evening hours. Deer are likely bedded in the cover you used to hide your approach in the morning, waiting for the sun to go down before moving out to feed. You should approach your stand through the field at this time of the day.

9. Guess a Deer's Sex by Analyzing Its Gait

You can tell buck tracks from doe tracks more easily when tracking deer through the snow. Does place their feet with precision; bucks sway from side to side while walking, a rolling gait that often leaves drag marks in powder. Longer drag marks may mean you've found the trail of an older or heavier buck.

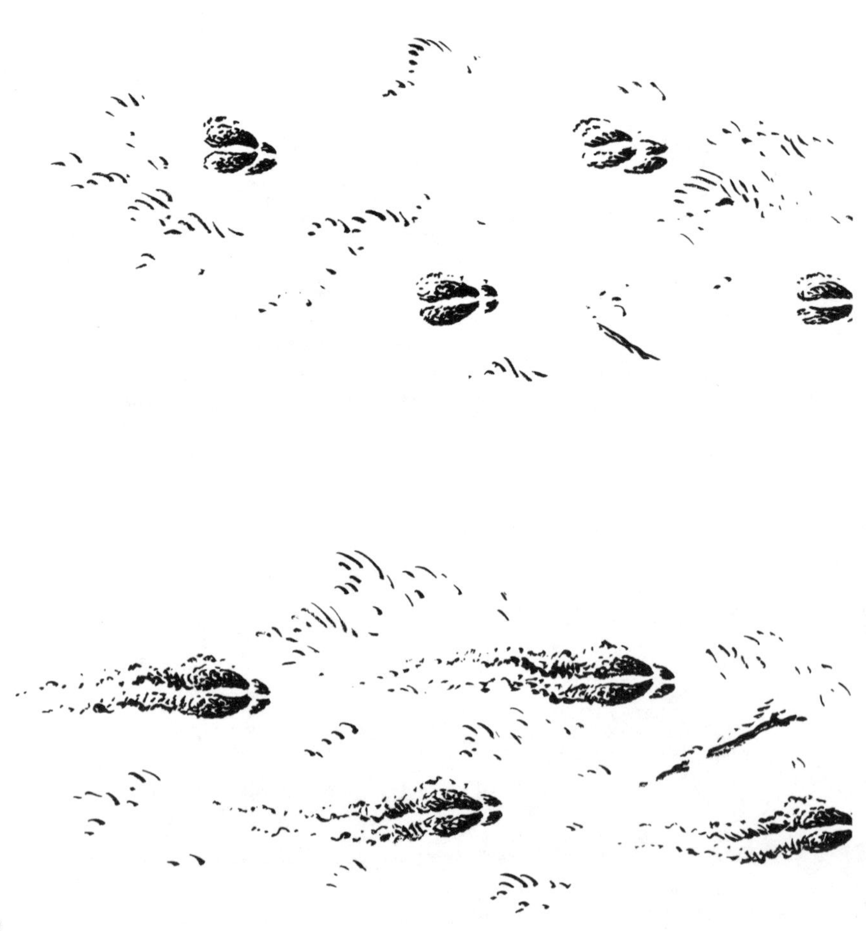

10. Hunt Near Food Sources When the Barometer Starts Dropping

White-tailed deer feed heavily in the days and hours leading up to the arrival of violent low-pressure systems. Watch your barometer. When the pressure starts dropping, head to the edges of crop fields and alfalfa meadows, or to stands of mature oak where the ground is covered with acorns. As the front gets closer, start hunting from stands set up along trails that lead from these food sources to heavy cover where you know deer go to hunker down during nasty weather.

11. Flush Big Bucks from beneath Downed Trees

When still-hunting through mature forest during hot weather, keep your eyes peeled for large trees that have been uprooted recently by storms. The maze of shade and cover offered by the fallen limbs and branches provides one of the best hiding places in the forest, and big bucks will often bed down deep within their embrace to escape the heat of the day. Experienced animals feel very secure in such cover and may not flush unless you get extremely close to them. Approach every such tree you can find.

12. Don't Get Too Hot to Sit Still in Cold Weather

When hiking out to your tree stand in cold weather, do not wear all the layers you'll need to stay warm while sitting still.

Doing so will cause you to sweat heavily on the way in, and this sweat will cool quickly once you stop moving, leaving you too chilled to remain quiet for long. Dress lightly and carry your outer layers in a backpack. Pull on warmer clothing only after you've climbed up into your stand and sat long enough for your heart rate to slow down.

13. Read Rub Lines to Anticipate a Buck's Movements at Different Times of the Day

Rubs can show you to where, at what time of the day, and in what direction a buck normally travels. When you first find a rub, get down on your knees so that your field of vision is similar to that of the buck that

made the rub. Scan for additional rubs in the area—chances are good you'll find another from thirty to fifty yards away. Repeat this process until you've identified a series of rubs, called a rub line. Rub lines often mark the routes a buck uses to travel to and from his preferred feeding and bedding areas. Most rubs in a line will be made on the same side of each tree; this tells you the direction the buck travels when using the route. If the line leads from a feeding area to thick bedding cover, set up a stand nearby and hunt there in the morning. If the line leads away from bedding cover, hunt it in the evening.

14. Hunt All Three Phases of the Rut

A good deer hunter knows that there is not just one rut, but three. The first, called the pre-rut, occurs in early October, when mature, four- and five-year-old does first come into estrus. The second, known as the peak or primary rut, runs from late October to the last week of November, and is when the majority of female deer come into heat. The third, called the post-rut or late rut, takes place twenty-eight days after the end of the primary rut, as does that were not bred during October and November come back into estrus. These pre- and post-rut phases do not last long. Look for a sudden explosion of fresh buck sign, then hunt hard for several days using techniques, such as rattling, that take advantage of the increased aggression triggered by competition for a limited number of willing does.

15. Gain Extra Seconds to Shoot When Rattling in a Buck

Bucks will often appear at the most inopportune moments, especially when you're rattling antlers to call them in. If you spot one while holding a rack in your hands, don't be afraid to put it down and pick up your gun. The buck you've called will be expecting to see some motion and will be less likely to startle immediately when he sees you, which gives you a few extra moments to shoot him. Using one smooth, unhurried motion, pick up your rifle, shoulder it, and fire. Make sure that you do not move too fast or jerk your arms, rifle, or body. Such sudden movements signal your excitement and may alarm the animal.

16. Let Blood Color Tell You How Fast to Follow a Wounded Buck

Blood trails don't just tell you the direction a wounded deer is moving. They can also provide good information about where on its body you shot the animal, and how quickly you should follow its trail. Bright red blood is full of oxygen and often means you've hit your deer in the lungs. Deer hit this way don't go far, so you can pursue them quickly. Dark red or purple blood may indicate a gut shot. If you find such blood, particularly in conjunction with bits of intestinal fat, and there's no precipitation forecast that could wash away or obscure the trail, consider giving the animal time to bed down and stiffen up before looking for a follow-up shot. Gut-shot deer often run long distances if they're chased immediately after being wounded.

17. Tie Back Branches When Hanging Your Tree Stand

While a good pair of pruning shears can be a bowhunter's best friend, there are many situations in which you should refrain from overclipping. For example, when setting up your tree stand, it is a good idea to try tying back any branches that obstruct your view, using a length of rope or wire. This method is quieter than clipping, will cause less damage to the tree you're using, and the branches can often be more easily positioned behind your stand in order to break up your silhouette.

18. Find Deer in Transition Zones

During the end of October and in early November, before the peak of the rut, deer switch from grazing in fields to browsing on twigs, branches, and buds. These foods are most easily found in wide transition zones of thick understory that grow up between mature forests and more open fields and meadows, where the shade cast by tall trees is not deep enough to inhibit the growth of younger saplings. The thick growth also serves as cover for the animals after leaves have fallen from the branches of more mature timber. Set your stand near deer trails close to rubs or scrapes in these transition zones, and you'll have a good chance of filling your tag.

19. Still-Hunt Uphill in the Early Morning

On calm days when there's little wind, air will flow downhill as it cools in the evening, and uphill as it heats up during the day. Deer use these currents to keep track of their surroundings. To keep them off your scent, hunt your way uphill in the late evening and early morning hours, and down during the rest of the day.

20. Hunt in Three Places at Once

One of the best locations to hunt is the intersection of three different types of vegetation. Look for a field corner bounded by timber on one side and a swamp, slough, or bottomland on the other, then hang your stand in a tree with a good view of any trails that lead from one to the other.

21. Don't Hang Your Stand Too High in Steep Terrain

While hanging your stand high in a tree will better hide your presence in level terrain, doing so in steep, hilly country may

actually put you at eye level with deer working down the ridges you're hunting. Try lowering your stand to camouflage your silhouette in such conditions. A deer looking downhill will have a more difficult time spotting you against a backdrop of leaf litter than it will spotting you against the sky.

22. Use Hunting Pressure on Public Land to Your Advantage

If you hunt public land that gets lots of pressure during the prime shotgun or rifle season, you're going to run into other hunters in the woods. Instead of letting them ruin your hunt, figure out how to use them to your advantage. Set your stand up on trails leading to thick cover near routes you know other hunters are using. Deer will flee to these areas when spooked by all the unusual sights, sounds, and smells in the woods, so you'll be in a good position to catch them as they sneak through.

23. A Basic Rule for Knowing When to Move and When to Sit Still

When you know deer are on the move, such as in the morning and evening hours, you should sit still in a good stand or other ambush point and wait for the animals to come to you. It is only during conditions in which deer stop moving that you should move to find them.

24. Develop a Quiet Stride for Still-Hunting

Maintaining proper balance is the key to walking quietly across the forest floor. A long stride combined with little forward momentum will often leave you tipping to one side or the other, which can force you to place your feet awkwardly as you catch your balance. To reduce the noise you make, learn to take smaller steps, and to place your feet heel or toe first. Shift your weight slowly onto your forward leg while rolling your foot from heel to toe (or toe to heel). When performed properly, this movement—called the rolling compression step—will allow you to feel any twigs, branches, or other objects that might make noise before you place your full weight on them. This lets you shift your weight to your back leg before the object snaps, then place your front foot in a new, less noisy spot.

25. Analyze Stomach Contents to Pattern Feeding Behavior

It's a good idea to examine the stomach contents of a deer you've shot. Less-digested food is what the deer ate last; well-digested food was eaten earlier in the day. You can use this information to guess where the deer was feeding in the hours before you killed it, and then apply what you've learned toward filling any open tags you or your buddies still have.

26. Easy Way to Check the Wind

Save a few of the black neck feathers from your next ruffed grouse—or the lightest feathers you can pick off doves,

pheasants, or quail if they're your favorite birds. Hung from a bow limb with a piece of dental floss, a light feather is a great wind direction indicator.

27. Don't Scare Big Bucks out of Bedding Sites

If you've located a good buck before the season, resist the urge to hunt him in his bedding site. This is almost certain to drive a wary trophy animal out of the area. Instead, hunt the travel zones between his bedding and feeding spots.

28. Gauge How Well Your Stand Is Hidden Using Black-and-White Images

A good way to tell if your stand or blind is well concealed is to photograph yourself sitting in it during the exact hours of the day you think you'll be hunting from it. Use a digital camera, and convert your images from color to black-and-white using the image-processing program on your computer. Deer are colorblind, so these black-and-white images will give you a good idea of the patterns, shapes, and tones that seem out of place. If you and your stand are easily recognizable, reconfigure its position and make sure that it is not too bright or too dark compared to its surroundings.

29. Practice with Your Bow in Hunting Situations

Always practice shooting your bow under the same conditions in which you expect to shoot your deer. You may be able to stick five arrows into a circle the size of your fist

at fifty yards when you're standing on flat ground and wearing a T-shirt, but that won't help you much if you don't know how to do the same thing while wearing a heavy jacket. Spend time during the preseason simulating live hunting situations. Use broadheads rather than field points, wear your hunting clothes, and practice shooting from awkward positions and elevat-ed angles.

30. Hunt Sleepy Bucks on Beds during a Full Moon

When the moon is full and the sky is clear, white-tailed deer will feed heavily during the evening hours and move less often during the day than they will when the sky stays dark all night. Run drives through heavy cover or still-hunt other likely bedding areas after a

well-lit night to increase your chances of filling your tag in such conditions.

31. Watch a Feeding Deer's Tail

Feeding deer always twitch their tails immediately before raising their heads to look around. If you immediately freeze when you see this motion, you'll be much less likely to alert the animal to your presence. Continue your stalk when the animal puts its head back down to feed.

32. Look Downhill When Still-Hunting during Bad Weather

The best places to still-hunt during violent weather are found on elevated terrain. Benches crossing the sides of ridges make excellent routes to follow because they give you top-down looks into the kinds of thick cover where deer like to hole up. That extra field of view means you'll have more shots than you would if you were stalking through level ground, where the cover you're hunting will usually obstruct your line of sight.

33. Don't Hang Your Stand Where You Find the Most Sign

Areas chock-full of deer trails, droppings, rubs, and beds are not always the best places to hang your stand. The abundance of sign could mean that the area is being used as a sanctuary—a place where deer congregate before heading out to feed, or where they bed down during the middle of the day. Since deer spend a great deal of time in such places, they become very familiar with them and will be sensitive to unusual sounds, smells, and sights. It can be extremely difficult to camouflage your presence under such conditions.

34. Bagging a Lunchtime Buck

Since most whitetail hunters are on their stands at first light, they tend to get restless from midmorning to noon. Many head back to camp, or their vehicles, seeking a sandwich and a chat with their buddies. That's when they inadvertently spook whatever deer are around, sending them sneaking away or bolting through the countryside. And that's exactly when hunters who have stayed on their stands, quiet and alert, reap the rewards of the biggest bucks.

35. Use a Stick to Track Wounded Game over Sandy Soil

Some soil types can absorb both tracks and blood, making trailing wounded deer difficult. If the trail you're following becomes indistinct, break off a straight stick that's the same length as the stride of the animal you're tracking. Place one end of the stick on the last clear track you can identify so that it's pointing in the direction you think the animal was traveling. Look for new tracks or flecks of blood at the other end.

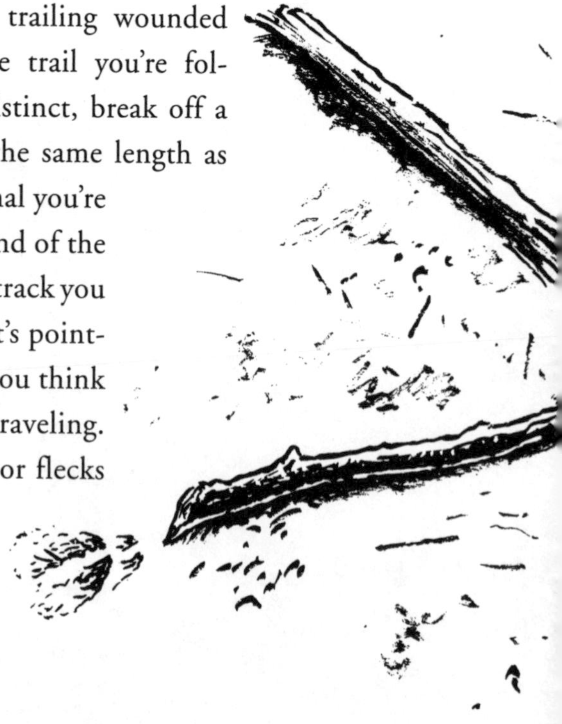

36. Sit Your Stand in the Morning When Hunting Hot Weather

Whitetails are more active than normal during the night when the weather is unseasonably warm, and will stay bedded down in well-shaded cover that's close to a water source during the heat of the day. They may start moving again as the temperature starts dropping early in the evening, but when it's really hot the air won't begin to cool until well after darkness. The best time of the day to hunt deer during hot weather is during the first two hours of shooting light in the morning, when the air is coolest and you can catch your quarry moving from where they've been feeding to where they'll bed during daylight.

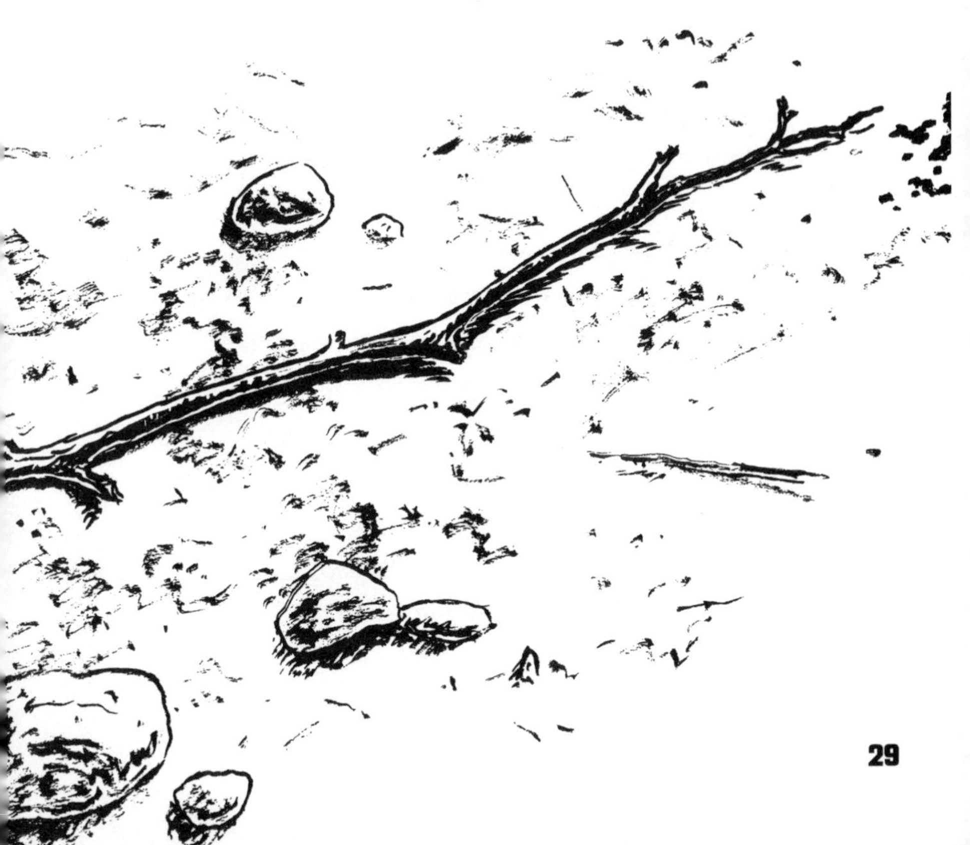

37. Any Buck Is a Good Buck!

In my personal opinion, the concept of hunting only trophy deer seems misguided for most hunters. If you get a kick out of it, fine. Have at it. Most hunters, however, simply want to get out to the deer woods with the idea of bringing home a buck, any buck. The bigger the buck, the more thrills we might feel. But in the end, the old deer-hunting bromide is so, so true: You can't eat horns. My advice is to relax, enjoy your hunting, and stick to the premise that any buck is a good buck.

38. Make Your Steps Sound like a Deer's to Spook Fewer Bucks

There are some situations in which it is impossible for you to walk silently through the woods. Dry leaves, for example, will crunch loudly no matter how carefully you place your feet. If you find it necessary to cover ground in such conditions (and there are no convenient game trails to follow that offer quieter places to walk), you will get closer to your quarry without spooking it if you learn how to pattern your steps so that they sound like the steps of a deer. Instead of a regular crunch, crunch, crunch, crunch, crunch (the standard human cadence), randomize the rhythm of your footsteps so that they form an erratic series of steps and pauses. Step, step, pause. Step. Pause. Wait. Step. Step. Step. Pause. And so on. You'll be much more likely to surprise bucks within shooting range if you use this pattern.

39. Spot Bucks Down Low

The horizontal line of a whitetail's back is one of the best things to look for when still-hunting through thick brush. Most lines in the woods are vertical, and while you'll eyeball a great many fallen logs by keying in on the horizontal lines, you'll have a better chance of locating a hidden deer this way than you would by looking for a whole animal. Remember, though, that even mature bucks stand only three feet at the shoulder, so don't raise your eyes any higher than this when scanning the area ahead of you.

40. Don't Face Your Stand at the Sun

When placing your tree stand, avoid setting it up so that it faces a rising or falling sun. The rays beaming directly into your eyes will make it harder for you to see into shadows during critical low-light hours, and will glance off glasses, gun barrels, and reflective items, spooking deer that would otherwise be unlikely to spot you.

CHAPTER 2

Elk Hunting

41. How to Field-Judge a Bull Elk

If you're looking for a trophy elk, you need to be able to quickly judge the quality of its antlers before taking a shot at the animal. You can do this in three steps. First, try to count the points. A true trophy will have no fewer than six points on each side. Second, gauge the length of each antler's beam. A

good bull should look as if it can tip back its head to scratch its rear end with the tips of his beams. Third, make sure that the bull's brow tines reach out over its muzzle, and that the other points have good length.

42. Don't Scout for Elk like You Scout for Deer

Unless you're hunting on private land, patterning an elk herd's activities before hunting season can be a waste of time. Elk react quickly to hunting pressure, and such pressure can be enormous on public lands, especially during the days leading up to the first of the season, when other hunters are out in force. Instead of scouting to identify a herd's normal, unstressed behaviors, focus your efforts on identifying where they go when spooked by the presence of other hunters. Look for heavy blowdown cover on steep slopes that are relatively close to meadows surrounded by thick timber. Elk feeding in these meadows will head toward such escape areas when startled. Identify good ambush sites along the likely routes they take, and you stand a good chance of shooting an animal pushed out by another hunter.

43. Don't Let Elk Spot You Twice in the Same Spot

If you notice an elk in the herd you're hunting suddenly stop chewing its cud to stare at your position, the ideal response is to immediately stop all movement, no matter how awkward the position you're in, and remain motionless until it turns its head away. There will be times, however, when it will be impossible to stay still long enough for the animal that's spotted you to lose interest. If you must move to a more comfortable position, your best option is to lower yourself as slowly as possible to the ground. Lie there as long as necessary, then crawl to a new position before raising your head to take stock of the situation. Even if the elk did not spook, it will still be monitoring the spot where it saw you move.

44. There's Only One Place to Shoot an Elk with a Bow

If you're hunting elk with a bow, the best shot to take is easy to remember, because there's only one ethical target to choose. Neck shots, shoulder shots, or shots at any

other part of an elk's body are not recommended; to kill an elk quickly with a bow, you must shoot it directly behind its shoulder, piercing its heart and/or lungs.

45. Secure Your Elk's Carcass on Steep Slopes

If an elk you've shot falls on the side of a steep slope, your first action after making sure the animal is dead should always be to secure the carcass to a solid anchor, such as a tree trunk, using a stout length of rope. The last thing you want is for the animal's body to slide downhill, which could damage the meat and/or put it at the bottom of a ravine where you'll have to work twice as hard to pack it out.

46. Catch Elk Moving from Their Food to Their Beds

The worst time to still-hunt for elk is at midday, when they will be bedded down in thick cover that they've chosen because it is impossible to approach without them seeing or smelling you. You'll have more luck spotting them before they spot you if you still-hunt during the early morning and late afternoon, when elk are moving from the meadows and clearings where they feed to the heavy evergreen cover where they often prefer to bed, and vice versa.

47. Bark like a Cow to Stop Startled Elk

You can briefly stop a spooked herd of elk by imitating the sound of a barking cow. A cow barks when she is alarmed. Other elk in the area will instinctively stop and look at her until she's identified the danger and run off, and then will follow her lead in exiting the area. If you're within range and have identified your target, use the moment when they stop and stare to take your shot.

48. Spot Late Season Bulls at High Elevation

Late in the season, you'll often find small groups of older bulls at higher elevations, where the snow is deep and the terrain is open. These bulls may be quite far from the rest of the herd, as much as a mile or more. Glass for them from below. When you spot such a group, try to pattern where the bulls feed and bed. Then set up a stalk to fit what you've observed. When planning your stalk, remember that if you spook the animals they will likely run to the nearest trees for shelter. If you're hunting in a group, post hunters along the tree line to intercept them.

49. How to Recognize Elk Tracks

Elk tracks look like very large deer tracks, and a mature bull's prints will be much larger than those left by female or juvenile elk. Make sure that you do not confuse elk tracks with those left by moose or cows. Cow tracks are rounded and do not look much like those of a deer, and moose tracks are longer and narrower than those left by elk. Study a guidebook (or this illustration) before you hunt to avoid this problem.

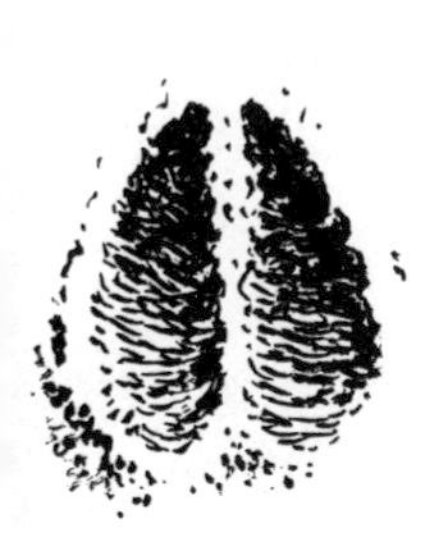
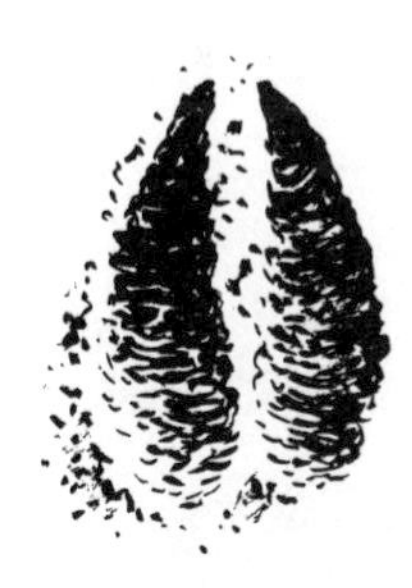
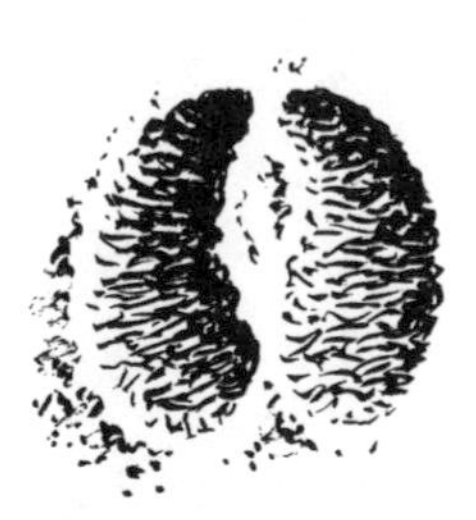

From left to right: bull elk, bull moose, cow elk, and juvenile elk tracks

50. The Top Ten Elk States (by Elk Population)

Colorado: 200,000
Montana: 150,000
Idaho: 140,000
Oregon: 106,000
Wyoming: 85,000
Washington: 60,000
Arizona: 55,000

Utah: 50,000
New Mexico: 45,000
California: 7,500

51. Keep Predators Away from Your Kill with a Smoky Fire

If you are hunting elk on foot and shoot one far from the road, you will have to make more than one trip to pack out the meat,

leaving the remaining meat alone in the backcountry. One way to keep bears, wolves, coyotes, and other predators from stealing your kill while you are away is to build a small, smoky fire from damp, pitchy wood near the quarters you had to leave behind. The smoke will help scare away predators, and you can use the plume to locate your kill quickly when you return to collect the rest of the animal. Make sure to do this only where

it's both legal and safe, and never leave a fire untended in dry conditions where there is any possible risk that it might spread.

52. Don't Bugle Too Often

A bugling bull makes an impressive sound, and one that's not hard to reproduce using today's commercial calls. Because of

this, and because many hunters have the unrealistic expectation that bulls often charge headlong toward the sound of a challenge, the bugle is the most overused call in an elk hunter's repertoire. Instead of relying on bugling to draw in a rutting bull, it's a better idea to use the call just to locate one, especially if you're hunting an area that gets lots of pressure. Once you've found a responsive bull, try to close with him by using other means. Call him in using cow calls, imitate the sounds of raking antlers, or even stalk silently downwind into shooting range.

53. Change Vantage Points to Fully Scope an Area

Don't dismiss an area as empty of game if you don't see any elk from a particular vantage point. You should always scope out an area from at least two positions so that you can view pockets and basins where elk may be feeding that are not easily identified from the beaten path. Changing vantage points takes work, and that's one reason why it can be such a successful tactic; most hunters won't be willing to make the effort and allow their desire for an easy hunt to let them dismiss an area before they've covered

it fully. Use this to your advantage when hunting on public land.

54. Approach Bedded Elk from Above

Elk like to bed in flat spots on side ridges where they can see well to the left, right, and downhill, and are high enough to feel comfortable that nothing will be approaching from behind. If you're fol-lowing one's track and it suddenly turns upslope, it could mean the elk is ready to bed. Avoid following its tracks any longer, as the animal will be paying close attention to its back trail. Instead, circle uphill, staying downwind of the trail, and try to approach where you think the elk has lain down from above.

55. Critical Advice to Elk Hunters

Calling elk in areas of heavy hunting pressure may be counterproductive. Bugling will draw other hunters, and bulls that have been called in and spooked wise up quickly. It is better to simply spot the bulls, then stalk them.

56. Look in Wet Meadows for Feeding Elk

Always pay close attention to wet meadows when looking for feeding elk. These small, moist clearings are rich in forbs and sedges, forage elk prefer. Wet meadows surrounded by thick timber are best; elk feeding in them will feel more secure when such cover is available, and will often feed later in the morning than they might in less accommodating terrain.

57. Call Back Elk from a Busted Herd

If you flush a herd of elk while still-hunting and it splinters into multiple groups, you can use the animals' desire to herd back up to call them to you. If the animals did not smell you when first flushed, they will slow down and take stock of the situation from a few hundred yards away. Get out your cow call and blow it softly, imitating the sounds other cows make when they're regrouping. If a cow answers you, answer back,

though wait for a few seconds first. If you do this right, the elk will think you're part of the group and will work back slowly in your direction.

58. It Takes Two to Tag a Called-In Elk

The textbook method of calling a bull into bow range requires two hunters. One serves as the caller, the other as the shooter. The shooter sets up in the shadows of a tree or some other type of cover with a good view of the path the bull should take. The caller sets up twenty to thirty yards upwind of the shooter. Since most bulls will approach the caller by circling downwind, they should appear directly in front of the shooter.

59. A Hot Weather Hot Spot for Daytime Elk

When the weather is hot, look for elk taking shelter in forests of mature evergreens that have few low branches. The forest canopy protects the animals from direct sunlight, while the open understory lets in cool breezes.

60. Find Elk in the Open after Bad Weather

Under most conditions, it is unusual to see elk feeding in the open during the middle of the day. The exception to this is if a period of strong winds or heavy rain or snow lets up at this time, or if the sun peaks through the clouds and warms up a slope that's been very cold. Elk will have been hunkered down,

waiting out the bad weather, and will often feed heavily for a few hours once conditions improve. These are great times to glass food sources, trails, and bedding cover for movement.

CHAPTER 3

Mule Deer Hunting

61. Let Low Light Show You Hidden Deer

The best time to glass for mule deer is as the sun first appears early in the morning. The low-angle light causes the hair on

their coats and light-colored rumps to glow, and will also gleam on the tines of a big buck's antlers. Low-angled evening light is also good for locating mule deer, but glassing in the late afternoon leaves you little time to stalk within range before the sun goes down.

62. Glass Your Route before You Stalk

Spotting mule deer is perhaps the easiest part of spot-and-stalk hunting. The stalk is just as important, and much more physically demanding. If you spot a bedded buck, don't immediately start moving into shooting range. First make sure that you're familiar with the route you're planning to take to get there. The best way to do this is to glass it thoroughly before packing up and moving out. Pick out landmarks you'll be able to identify (look for ones that can be recognized from multiple angles), and make sure to remember where they are in relation to where the animal is bedded down. Start your stalk once you've established a clear mental picture of the path you think will put you in a downwind location with a clear shot at the buck.

63. Meandering Tracks Mean Beds Are Close

If a mule deer is traveling from a food source to bedding cover its trail will generally lead in a straight line (taking terrain into account). But as the animal approaches its bedding site it often starts to meander through the cover, nibbling on twigs and looking for a spot to lie down. If you're tracking a muley and see its trail start to wander, turn around and backtrack for a few hundred yards, then climb above where you think the animal has bedded down so that you can approach from a higher elevation. You'll get closer to the deer and will have a better shot at the animal if you spook it.

64. Don't Shoot Deer You Can't Reach

One of the worst mistakes a mule deer hunter can make is shooting a buck on the other side of a ravine or canyon without knowing whether it's possible to retrieve the animal. Vertical cliffs, deep rivers, and maze-like canyons are difficult obstacles to negotiate, and some are impossible to cross. Make sure you know the terrain you're hunting before you take a shot like this.

65. Mule Deer Prefer Sagebrush

If you're hunting in unfamiliar territory, one of the best places to look for muleys is in thick patches of sagebrush. Mule deer seem to prefer this plant throughout their range. Pay special attention to patches you find in places where sagebrush is relatively rare; the plant will act like a magnet for muleys in the area.

66. Get in a Mule Deer's Zone

According to Dennis Wintch, mule deer editor for *Hunting Illustrated* magazine, most mule deer habitat can be broken up

into three distinct zones: a high zone (8,000 to 12,000 feet), a middle zone (5,000 to 8,000 feet), and a low zone (1,000 to 5,000 feet). Mule deer cycle through these zones depending on weather, hunting pressure, and food availability. The trick is to figure out which zone they're currently inhabiting. If you're hunting in a new area, look for fresh tracks and follow them until you're confident you know which level the deer are currently using.

67. Getting the Range Right under the Big Sky

The most difficult adjustment easterners make when hunting the West for the first time is adjusting to the scale of thing. Deer tend to be significantly larger than what East Coasters are used to. Elk are five or six times better. Guesstimating ranges is a real crap shoot. Better depend on a rangefinder when hunting the wide-open spaces.

68. Catch Bucks Seeking Shade in the Middle of the Day

While the most productive times to glass for mule deer will be during first hours of morning and the last hours of the day, you can still spot deer moving during the middle of the day if you know where to look. Bucks will often change bedding sites during the middle of the day as shade shifts with the sun's movement, sometimes browsing for a few minutes before they lay down again. You'll be most likely to catch this movement if you're already glassing cover for bedded deer. Look under trees

and around brush for anything that seems out of place with it surroundings. When a buck stands up you'll be focused in the right place.

69. Tag Team a Spot-and-Stalk

One of the best ways to stalk within range of a bedded mule deer is to leave a hunting partner

behind at the place you first spotted the animal. Your partner can then use hand signals to guide you as you sneak into shooting range. He'll need to far enough away from the bedded deer to not startle it when moving his hands, so bring a pair of binoculars and use them to check on him for instructions at regular intervals.

70. Let the Wind Settle into One Direction

Wind currents can be fickle before the sun rises, so it's a good idea to wait until later in the morning before planning a stalk on a buck you've spotted. In most open-country habitat, the wind will usually settle as the air heats up, blowing in a consistent direction that makes staying downwind of your target much simpler.

71. Don't Let Your Bow Keep You from Creeping on Your Stomach

Creeping to within shooting range of an open-country mule deer is one of the most difficult and exciting challenges in all of bowhunting, especially when there's only an open stretch of tall grass between you and the buck you're stalking. To close with your target in such terrain you'll need to inch forward on your stomach, keeping your head down and using only your elbows to pull yourself forward. But it can be difficult to remain silent

when you're carrying a bulky, awkward bow in your hands. You can keep your arms moving freely by placing the bow on your back. When you're close enough to shoot, simply slide the bow into your hands, knock an arrow, sit up on your knees, and shoot quickly.

72. Glass for Bucks in Comfort

It is very important that you situate yourself comfortably when glassing for mule deer. Choose a place to sit that has a solid back support, such as a big rock or a stump, and bring foam pad, or, if you can spare the weight, a small, folding tripod stool to keep your butt off cold, hard ground. You should also invest in a tripod with adjustable legs for your binoculars and/or spotting scope, which will reduce the strain on your arms. Never spot for deer with your rifle scope; you'll end up pointing the muzzle of your gun at targets you do not want to shoot.

73. Stalk When the Wind Blows Strongly

If you spot a buck bedded in grassy, open terrain, wait to stalk it until the middle of the day, when the wind usually blows steadiest and strongest. The strong wind will wave grass, leaves, and branches back and forth, and you can use these natural movements to camouflage your progress into shooting position. Wear a ghillie suit for further protection from a mule deer's sharp eyes; the loose strips of fabric attached to the suit will move with the wind, making you look that much more like a part of the landscape.

74. Use the Right Binocular/Spotting Scope Combination

Large, 11x80 or 20x80 binoculars of the type designed for stargazers make excellent mule deer spotting tools because they gather a great deal of light, giving you an excellent picture during the twilight hours, which is when most muleys will be moving. But if you're hiking long distances to reach your hunting areas, you won't want to carry such heavy glass. A good compromise is to use a smaller pair of 10x50 binoculars and also bring a small, 20- or 25-power spotting scope. The combined weight of both these optics will be less than the weight of the larger binoculars, and you can break the weight up by storing your scope in your pack as you hike. Use the binoculars to spot movement at long range, then use the scope to get a closer look at whatever caught your attention.

75. Be Prepared to Hike Long Distances

Always wear a daypack when you hunt mule deer. You often have to cover long distances to find them in the open country they live in, and you don't want to get stuck far from your truck without the proper equipment when the weather changes suddenly, as it often does in the mountains. Make sure your pack fits well and is roomy enough to carry a change of clothes, rain gear, a good knife, rope, binoculars, a compass, a survival kit, and extra food and water. Bring your pack even when you think you'll be hunting close to your camp or your vehicle; you never know when a fresh track might take you deep into the backcountry.

76. Locate Clear-Cuts to Find Feeding Mule Deer

One of the best places to hunt mule deer in evergreen forest habitat is a recently logged clear-cut. Deer-friendly shrubs and plants grow rapidly in these clearings as their roots penetrate the disturbed soil and their leaves soak up sunlight normally blocked by large trees. You may have to walk a few miles to reach such clear-cuts, as most logging roads on public lands will be closed to public vehicle traffic, but with unpressured, top-notch feeding habitat as your reward, the hike will be worth the effort. Contact your local BLM or Forest Service office to get information on where these cuts have taken place (you want cuts that are 10 years old or younger), and plan your hunt accordingly.

77. Use Thermal Currents When Stalking Bedded Bucks

Early morning air that has been cooling all night tends to flow downhill; later in the morning, as this air heats up in the light of the sun, it will reverse direction. These uphill/downhill flows are called thermal currents, and they are important to remember when stalking hot-weather bucks. If you're glassing a clearing for feeding deer at first light, make sure you're positioned so that no downhill currents will carry your scent to the animals. Later, as the deer move uphill to bed, plan your stalk so that you approach them from above.

78. Look for Bucks in Edge Cover on the North Sides of Ridges

A great place to look when you're spotting for bedded mule deer is edge cover (thick brush lining clearings or other openings in which deer can remain concealed while still enjoying a good view of their surroundings). Look first along the north sides of ridges, which generally get more shade. Since deer here will already be bedded down, try to pick out pieces of the animals. Ear flicks, hind-leg scratches, and antler-glints may be the only clues you'll have to find the buck you're hunting.

79. See and Be Seen

When glassing for mule deer, keep in mind that if you're sitting in a place with a 360-degree view of the surrounding terrain, deer on all sides will have a good view of you, as well. Make sure to hide your silhouette by sitting with a rock, some brush, or a stump at your back.

80. Follow the Farthest Track

Mule deer are very alert to the sounds and smells of animals following their back trails and will spook easily if they see you before you see them. To make sure you get the drop on an animal you're tracking, avoid looking too closely at its individual prints. Instead, keep track of the overall trail by picking out the furthest clear track you can see, then still-hunting up to it, keeping your eyes peeled for movement in the distance. Repeat until you find your target.

CHAPTER 4

Bear Hunting

81. How to Tell a Grizzly Bear from a Black Bear before Taking a Shot

When hunting bears in the western states you must be very good at distinguishing between black bears, which are huntable, and grizzlies, which are protected under federal law. Color is not a determining characteristic; many black bears exhibit the same blonde coloration often associated with grizzly bears, and many grizzly bears come in darker colors. Instead, a hunter

should look for two things. The first is the presence of a distinct hump on the shoulders; grizzlies have one, black bears do not. A hunter should also try to get a good look at the animal's face in profile. A black bear's nose slopes down from its forehead in a straight line. A grizzly bear's forehead dips inward from the forehead before pushing out into its nose, giving its face an indented, slightly concave appearance.

82. A Bear of Many Colors

Not all black bears are black. They come in many color phases, including blonde, cinnamon, chocolate, and even pure white or blue. Hunt the eastern states if you want a black phase black bear; other color phases are rare east of the Mississippi. Hunt the western states for a brown, cinnamon, or blonde-phase black bear. White phase bears (known as Kermode or spirit bears) and blue phase bears (known as Glacier bears) are found in British Columbia, but are protected from hunting by law in the province. Glacier bears, however, are also found in Alaska and can be hunted there.

83. Look for Crop-Raiding Bears

If you live in a state that will not allow you to hunt bears over bait, you'll need to figure out where the animals are naturally feeding. One easy way to do this is to canvas farmers in the area you're hunting to see if any of them are having problems with bears raiding their corn fields, gardens, or other crops. You'll get a head start on the scouting process, and get the added bonus of expanding the amount of land on which you have permission to hunt.

84. The Best Time for Bear Pelts

The earlier in the spring you can shoot a bear, the better quality its hide will be. Bears shed their winter coats as the weather warms up, often rubbing against trees, rocks, and fence posts to scrape off unwanted hair. If you shoot one later in the spring it may have a patchy, scruffy-looking hide. Catch them close to when they leave their dens you'll get a much better-looking pelt.

85. When Black Bears Attack

"Indian hunters will tell you that a fighting black is more to be feared than either the grizzly or Kodiak, for the reason that the latter two species seem always to be in a frantic hurry about mauling a man, while a black will rip and tear at a victim as long as there is a spark of life remaining. This explanation of the Kodiak's tactics may account for the number of men who have lived to tell the tale after being mauled by the big brownies."

—Russell Annabel, "Plenty of Bear," *Field & Stream*, 1937, reprinted in *The Field & Stream Reader*, Doubleday, 1946

86. The Curious Eating Habits

"Black bear generally feed on berries, nuts, insects, carrion, and the like; but at times they take to killing very large animals. In fact, they are curiously irregular in their food. They will kill deer if they can get at them; but generally the deer are too quick. Sheep and hogs are their favorite prey, especially the latter, for bears seem to have a special relish for pork. Twice I have known a black bear to kill cattle."

—Theodore Roosevelt, *The Wilderness Hunter*, 1893

87. Tell Black Bear Tracks from Grizzly Tracks

You can't tell a black bear's tracks from a grizzly's based on size alone. Large black bears will have tracks as big as medium-size grizzlies, and variations in sex and age make this an even more unreliable indicator. And while grizzlies usually have longer claws than black bears (translating into claw marks further from the tips of the toe imprints), not all surfaces pick up claw marks. The best way to tell which animal left a track you've found is this: find the imprint of the bear's front foot and draw a straight line across the base of the toes so that it's just touching the top of the front pad. If it's a grizzly track, most of the toes will be above this line. If it's a black bear the inside toe will be mostly below this line.

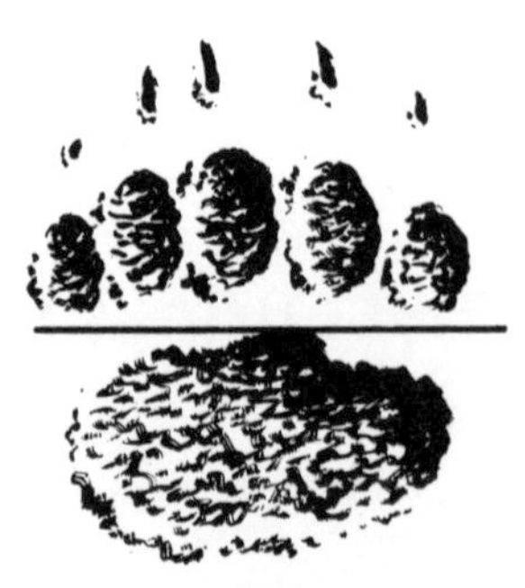

88. The Differences between Boars and Sows

It can be very difficult to determine the sex of a black bear in the field. Male black bears, called boars, are generally much larger than females (sows) and have larger heads and longer bodies. Female bears rarely reach 350 pounds; boars commonly grow to 500 pounds or more. However, the only sure way to tell a younger male from a female is to look for a penis. This is easy in the spring and summer months, but can be difficult in the fall, when a bear's belly hair will be quite long.

89. Why Late Season Is a Great Season

Fall bear hunting generally gets better later in the season. One reason is that bears move more often in cooler weather. Another is that in states or provinces where baiting is legal, hunters will often stop maintaining their bait piles after they fill their tags. Animals that were feeding on such bait will actively search for new food sources, making your own pile that much more attractive. Last, if you kill a bear in the late season, when the air is usually cold, you'll have an easier time of getting your meat out of the woods before it sours.

90. Carry Tracking Line to Mark a Blood Trail

According to Richard P. Smith, author of *The Book of the Black Bear*, one of the best ways to keep track of a bear's blood trail is to carry a couple of spools of Game Tracker line. This line is more

commonly used by bowhunters (it attaches to their arrows and spools out after they shoot) but is also very helpful for hunters carrying guns. If you're trailing a wounded bear, simply allow the tracking line to pay out behind you. You'll get an easy to follow, continuous record of the trail you're following, and you won't have to break your concentration in order to tie bits of surveyors tape to branches or mark the trail some other way.

91. Size a Bear by Looking at Its Tracks

You can get a good idea of how large a bear is by looking at its tracks. Average-sized black bears

(150 to 200 pounds, dressed) will leave front tracks that are 3½ to 4 inches wide, and rear tracks that are from five to six inches long. The tracks left by a trophy-sized animal will be much larger, with front pads five to six inches wide, and rear pads eight inches or longer.

92. Talk Loudly to Avoid Startling Bears

According to Richard P. Smith, author of *The Book of the Black Bear*, a hunter should rarely sneak when hiking in to hunt a bait pile. If a bear is already feeding there, the sudden appearance of a human may startle the animal, which could cause it to avoid the bait in the future, or to feed on it only at night. Instead, the hunter should warn any bears in the area of his approach well in advance of arriving at the bait. Whistle and talk in a normal, calm voice on the way in; this will notify the bear that you're on your way before you're close enough to startle the animal. Bears know that bait is left by humans and while they will move away off to avoid being seen when they hear people approaching, they will not be spooked as long as they are not taken unawares, and should return once they think you are no longer in the area.

93. Give a Bear Time to Die

Be careful when trailing a bear you've shot if you're only hunting with a bow. Pay attention to where your arrow hits the animal, and delay tracking it until you're confident that the bear has had time to die. Wait at least a half an hour if you hit it in the lungs, an hour if you hit it in the liver, and at least four hours if you shoot it in the gut. If possible (and legal), bring along a friend with a gun.

94. What a Bear Trail Looks Like

Because bears will generally step in the exact same places when taking familiar routes, well-used bear trails often look like old, deep footprints worn into the forest floor rather than the smooth, groove-like paths normally associated with game trails.

95. Trail a Drive to Bag a Trophy

One of the best ways to bag a big bear when putting on a drive through thick cover is to post a couple of shooters behind the drivers. Older bruins do not startle easily and will avoid leaving their security cover if at all possible. Instead of running out ahead of the drivers as a younger bear might do, a big bruin will often simply circle around them. Hunters following the drive stand a good chance of seeing bears that behave this way.

96. Bowhunting Black Bears

Time was when only the top experts even thought about taking a bear with a bow. Not today. Many of the same bowhunters who bag whitetail bucks with their bows are on the hunt for black bears—mostly over bait in Canada. Opportunities to bag a bear with a bow abound in Canada. When Googling for information, make sure you type in the province you're interested in, and, of course, look for the guides and outfitters who have solid records in bowhunting.

97. How to Measure a Trophy Bear

"Boone & Crockett recognizes four species of bear in North America: the Alaska brown bear, the grizzly bear, the black bear, and the polar bear. All are scored the same way, by measuring a dry skull's greatest width and adding it to its greatest length. The minimum scores required to make the all-time B&C books are:

Alaska brown bear—28 inches
Polar bear—27 inches
Grizzly bear—24 inches
Black bear—21 inches."

—Tom McIntyre, www.fieldandstream.com

98. Where to Shoot a Bear with a Gun

The best place to shoot a black bear with a rifle, shotgun, or handgun when the animal is broadside to you is directly in the center of its shoulder. If you're using the right caliber rifle (.270 or higher) this shot should break both of the animal's shoulders and penetrate its lungs. If the bear is facing you the best place

to shoot it will be directly in the center of the chest. If it's facing away from you, shoot it in the center of its back, directly between the shoulder blades.

99. Use Multiple Knives When Trimming Bear Fat

Bears spend the summer and fall months building up a thick layer of fat in preparation for their winter dormancy. If you shoot one in the fall, you'll need to trim off this fat before storing the animal's meat. The meat will keep longer and take up less space in your freezer, but the process takes time. Save some by having a few spare knives and a sharpening tool handy.

100. Don't Plan a Spring Hunt Too Early

Watch the weather when planning a spring bear hunt. A warm spring will get bears moving earlier in the season, but an unseasonably cold one will discourage them from leaving their dens. If you're traveling out west or to Canada to hunt spring bears, it's a good idea to build a bit of cushion into your schedule in case winter lingers longer than normal.

CHAPTER 5

Pig Hunting

101. Distinguish Hog Tracks from Deer Tracks

Although hog tracks and deer tracks can be the same size, it is not difficult to tell them apart once you know what to look for. Hog tracks are blockier than deer tracks and have rounded rather than pointed tips. Deer tracks are teardrop shaped; hog tracks are square in both front and back, and have a more uniform width.

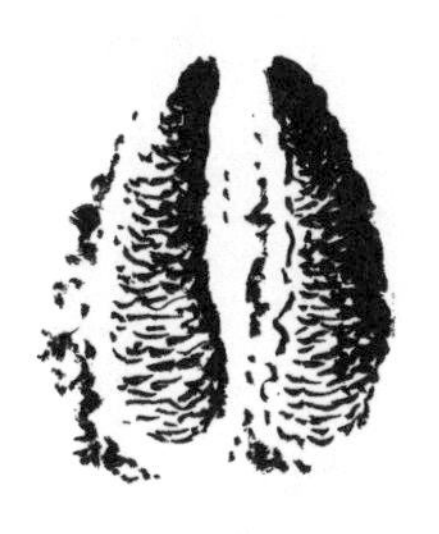

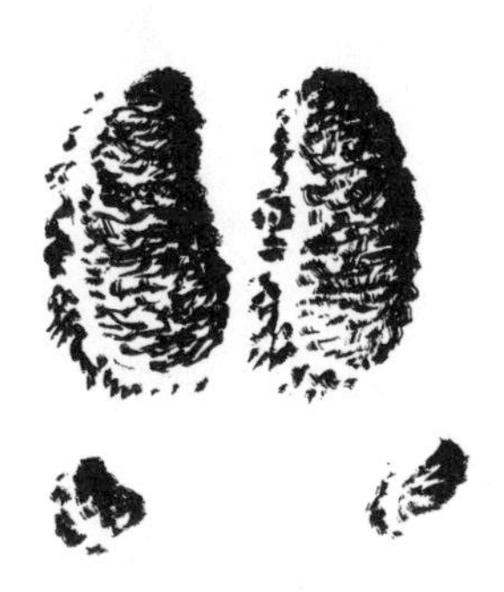

102. Hunt Small Herds to Find Unpressured Pigs

If you know there are pigs in the area you're hunting but find only minimal amounts of sign, do not get discouraged. Smaller herds of pigs can be more predictable (and thus easier to hunt) because they are generally less pressured than larger groups, whose obvious trails and numerous wallows attract many more hunters.

103. Wild vs. Feral

Very few of the hogs in North America are truly wild—most are descended from domestic pigs, and should be referred to as feral. A true Russian wild boar has a much longer nose and legs than a hog descended from domestic stock, it will have a pronounced ridge of hair running down the center of its back, and its tail will be straight.

104. Shoot to Kill Quickly When Hunting Hogs

A hog's vital organs are located lower in its body cavity than are vital organs in the body cavities of ungulates. To ensure a killing shot, always aim directly behind the shoulder as well as slightly lower than you would aim on a white-tailed deer. Be very sure of your shot before pulling the trigger or releasing your arrow. You do not want to have to follow one far after hitting it; hogs have a thick layer of fat beneath their skin that can quickly plug a wound, making blood trailing difficult, especially if you shoot the animal in a wet, swampy environment.

105. Spot-and-Stalk Hogs in Open Country

In fairly open country, spotting wild pigs from a distance and then stalking them can be an effective method. Start out by trying

to situate yourself you where you have a commanding view and the wind is coming toward you. If pigs are seen at a distance, walk slowly and quietly toward them, keeping the wind at your face and using available cover. Since wild pigs have poor eyesight, you may be able to get fairly close without being detected.

—www.jesseshunting.com

106. Look for Thickets to Find Bedded Pigs

Wherever you hunt pigs, you can be confident that they'll spend their days holed up in the thickest vegetation to be

found. Look for palmetto thickets in swampy bottomland, laurel tangles in the mountains, and grown-over clear cuts in forested country that are near a good source of food, such as

an old orchard or grove of acorn-producing oaks. Set up your stand on trails that lead from their bedding cover to where they eat and make sure you're sitting in it long enough for the scent you left on the way in to disperse by the time they head out to feed in the evening.

107. Here He Comes!

"When a wild boar means mischief, he makes his run with his head down. It is by a sudden thrust upward of his tusks that he does his deadly work. When he charges with his head high, he probably means that he just wants gangway."

—Archibald Rutledge, *An American Hunter,* Lippincott, 1937

108. Look for Wallows When Scouting for Hogs

Wallows are muddy or dusty patches of ground where pigs roll to cool themselves off, remove parasites attached to their skin, and cover themselves in dirt to keep off biting insects. These are great places to look for when scouting, because you can use them to identify the sizes and numbers of animals in a herd. Tracks are easy to find in such places, and you can get an accurate read on a hog's size by measuring the imprints left by its body in the mud.

109. Wild Boars: What You're Hunting

Wild boars in America are a mixture of feral (born wild) pigs from domesticated stock running loose in the woods for decades, even centuries, and of original European wild boars brought into this country and planted at different locations. One of the main plantings was by a man named George Moore who in 1912 put fourteen European wild boars on his 1600 acres of timbered land surrounding Harper's Bald, a mountain peak in the Snowbird Mountain Range of North Carolina. Moore thought of his land as a preserve, but, of course, the hogs roamed into the countryside and have been there for decades, plus spreading elsewhere in the Great Smokies. The

pure European wild boars have also been imported in places ranging from New Hampshire to California to Georgia.

110. Hunt Hogs near Old Homesteads

One of the best places to look for wild hogs is around an abandoned homestead. Pigs like these sites because they often contain abandoned orchards, overgrown gardens with wild-growing vegetables, and are located close to open meadows or overgrown pasture that offer a range of other food sources.

CHAPTER 6

Moose Hunting

111. Don't Glass from the Same Spot You Call

It's always a good idea to change your location after you've finished an extended calling sequence so that you are glassing the area from a spot upwind of where you were calling. If there's a bull in the area, you can be sure he will have heard you and will remember the exact spot your calling came from. When he eventually comes in to investigate it's likely he'll first circle downwind of where he heard your calls. Switching spots lets you stay undetected if this happens.

112. Be Patient When Calling in Moose

Moose are curious creatures, but they can take their time satisfying that curiosity. Even during the peak of the rut it can take days for a moose that's heard your calling to decide to investigate. Be patient. There will be rare occasions when a nearby bull that's crazed with lust comes crashing into your setup right away, but most calling won't pay off until many hours later.

113. Walk like a Moose

Moose have sensitive ears and a keen sense of smell. It is very unlikely you'll be able to approach one on foot without it hearing you, even if you're working into the wind. Fortunately, you do not have to be completely silent. Instead, try to sound like a moose. First, make sure you're wearing no clothing that makes unnatural rustling sounds when brushed against branches or grass. Second, make sure any metal items you're carrying in your pockets, on your gun sling, or clipped to your jacket or pants are tightly secured so that they don't clink or clank while you're walking. Last, do not try to sneak. Predators sneak, tensing up their bodies in order to perform deliberate movements designed to minimize motion and reduce the sounds of their steps. Moose know what sneaking sounds like, and most humans are not capable of sneak quietly enough to fool one. You'll have more luck if you step as quietly as possible while still maintaining a loose, natural stride. Any sounds you make will likely be mistaken for the sounds of another moose, elk, or deer moving at a relaxed pace through the brush.

114. How to Recognize a Pissed-Off Moose

When a moose is irritated by your presence, it will use its body language to warn you that it's upset, pulling its ears back and flaring the long hair along its neck and hump, much the way a dog will when looking for a fight. It may even growl at you and lick its lips. When you see this, back away quickly and try to get a large obstruction between you and the animal.

115. Russell Annabel on Alaska Moose Hunting

"Sheep hunting is great sport, bear hunting is packed with adventure and thrills, and there is a definite kick in risking your neck climbing the windy crags of the goat country—but for downright fun, I'll take a moose hunt any old time. Like grouse shooting, it's a sport that goes with bright leaves tingling down through the branches of old trees, with quiet noonday watches on sun-drenched hillsides, with cautious sallies through the shadowy green-gold enchantment of deep forest aisles, and with campward horseback rides in the purple, star-shot dusk of mountain evenings. It is a sport for the man who appreciates the

wilderness at its best, who has an eye for color and beauty—and yet it also has its taut, pulse-quickening moments."

—Russell Annabel, "In the Moon of the Painted Leaves," *Field & Stream,* 1936, reprinted in *The Field & Stream Reader,* Doubleday, 1946

116. When to (and When Not to) Use a Big Scope

Oversize, 50mm objective lenses will always collect more light than standard-size rifle scopes, giving you a distinct advantage in low-light conditions—brighter, sharper images of the animals you're aiming at. This does not mean, however, that you should always carry such a scope on your rifle. Oversize

lenses are great choices if you're hunting from a stand or spotting and stalking in country where you expect to take long shots at unsuspecting moose. But if you plan to do much still-hunting, they can be a liability. There are two reasons for this.

The first is that oversize scopes require higher mounts than standard scopes, which means it's more difficult to acquire a proper sight picture when you need to make a quick shot. The

second is that oversized scopes are heavy! You'll be much happier if you mount standard-sized optics on the gun you use for still-hunting.

117. Moose Hunting in a Big Wind

Upland bird hunters hate days of the howling winds. Duck hunters love them. Moose hunters should love them. Working your way into position for a shot at moose is much easier in a big wind, if you plan your hunt to approach from downwind. First, the moose isn't going to catch your scent. Secondly, they can't hear much with the wind howling.

118. Moose by Canoe

Moose love water, and so do many moose hunters. This is because there are few ways to access unpressured moose habitat more quietly and with less effort than by paddling into it. And there are few ways of packing out moose meat more efficiently than by carrying its quarters in a canoe. Scan banks

and shorelines for moose standing hidden in the brush, and pay close attention when paddling up or floating down rivers that connect ponds and small lakes—moose travel along these streams because they often flow through flat terrain that's easier for them to traverse.

119. Call like a Cow Using Only Your Voice

Cow calls are high-pitched groans that can be best described as a high, moaning "eerrrrrrrr" sound. These calls can be relatively short in duration, or can last for up to two minutes. You can imitate the sound using your voice alone. To do so, pinch your nose (a nasal sound does a better job of imitating a cow), cup your hands over your mouth, and start your "err" sound at a lower pitch, gradually raising pitch in the middle of the call, holding the "r," and wavering your tone a bit before lowering the pitch as you taper off into silence.

120. Stop a Startled Bull with a Cow Call

If you spook a bull, try making a long, loud cow call as he runs away. There's a good chance he'll stop to figure out where the sound is coming from, giving you an opportunity to make a quick shot.

CHAPTER 7

Caribou Hunting

121. Caribou Migrate the Furthest

Some caribou migrate more than 3,000 miles each year—farther than any other land animal. They travel in herds every fall and spring from their wintering to their calving grounds, and arrive just in time to think about heading back.

122. Multi-Purpose Hooves

A caribou's hooves are wide, concave, and act like snowshoes, distributing the animal's weight on snow, ice, and melted muskeg. These hooves also work like paddles when caribou need to swim across fast-flowing rivers, or even large lakes. But they don't slow the animals down. Caribou have been recorded running faster than 50 miles per hour.

123. Caribou Never Stop Moving

Caribou are not the wiliest game animals a man can hunt, but that doesn't make them easy prey. First you have to find them.

Then you have to decide whether or not to wait to shoot a trophy. You can't pattern a caribou because it never stays in one place. The herd you're stalking today might be miles and miles away the next. If you see a bull you like, pull the trigger, because you never know what tomorrow will bring.

124. Bring the Right Optics

Unless you're a bush pilot, hardest part of hunting caribou will be finding the herd. Bring high-power binoculars (at least 10 × 42) and carry a spotting scope. Make sure to use top-quality glass or you'll lose your ability to hunt during the morning and evening hours.

125. Don't Spook the Herd

"When you're sneaking up on a bull, keep track of other caribou. They seem to float in from nowhere just when you want to move. Though caribou won't jet away like a whitetail buck when you surprise them at a distance, they will jog off and take other caribou with them. Then you have two options: Stay put and hope they stop so that you can stalk them again, or run after them. In my experience, spooked caribou seldom give you an easy second hunt."

—Wayne van Zwoll, "Caribou: Noble and Mobile," www.fieldandstream.com

126. How to Field-Judge a Caribou's Antlers

When trying to guess the length of a caribou's antlers, use the animal's shoulder as a measuring stick. Most shoulders will be between 48 and 54 inches high. Look for antlers with curved main beams, which will generally be both longer and wider than straight ones (though they may look shorter from the side). A trophy animal's shovels will be broad, have multiple points, and extend far out over the muzzle. Kicker points, the spikes that grow off the back of a caribou's antlers, will add to the score, as will palmation and extra points at the tops.

127. How to Read a Caribou's Body Language

"When caribou are not alarmed, they walk quite slowly, extending the head forward and downward. When alarmed, caribou perform a special behavior to warn other caribou of danger. They'll do this if a predator gets too close, but isn't about to catch them (or after they figure out that you're a person sitting on a rock). An alarmed caribou will trot with the head held high and parallel to the ground, and the short, normally floppy tail held up in the air."

—Alaska Department of Fish and Game

128. A Good Gun for Caribou

While a good shot won't need more than a .270 to take down a thin-skinned animal like a caribou, the animals are much larger-bodied than most whitetail deer. It can help to shoot a bigger gun when you're reaching out to knock one down at the long ranges you'll often find when hunting in the tundra. One great caribou cartridge is the .338 Win Mag. Loaded with a

200-grain bullet, the cartridge will hit three inches high at 100 yards. Elmer Keith loved this chambering for both caribou and elk, and you will, too.

129. Winterize Your Caribou Gun

Always make sure to keep your gun clean, moisture-free, and either grease-free or treated with synthetic lube designed to function in extreme freezing temperatures. The last thing you want when firing your rifle at a caribou after a long, freezing, late season stalk is for the hammer, firing pin, or trigger to malfunction because your gun's oil congealed in the cold.

130. Don't Put Wet Bullets into a Freezing-Cold Rifle

Always carefully clean any cartridges you've dropped on the ground if you're hunting in the far north during the late season. They make pick up moisture that causes them to freeze to the inside your gun's chamber, reducing your expensive rifle to a single-shot firearm.

CHAPTER 8

Pronghorn Antelope Hunting

131. Vision and Speed: The Pronghorn's Defense

"His eye is larger than that of cow or horse, nearly as large as that of an elephant; they give him somewhat the appearance of

a huge beetle. He can see half or three-quarters of a mile away, with a range of vision keener than that of an 8-power glass. . . . I've seen a herd fairly fly across the plains up to the foothills and trees, then scorn the cover they have reached and circle back and back again, as if playing a game of tag with your bullets. The pronghorn is a real sportsman. He runs, but he never hides."

—Major Robert E. Treman, "Wyoming Antelope," *Field & Stream,* 1937, reprinted in *The Field & Stream Reader,* Doubleday, 1946

132. The Pronghorn Challenge

"Antelope shooting is the kind in which a man most needs skill in the use of the rifle at long ranges; they are harder to get near than any other game—partly from their wariness and still more from the nature of the ground they inhabit . . . Even good hunters reckon on using six or seven cartridges for every prong-horn they kill; for antelope are continually offering standing shots at very long distances, which, nevertheless, it is a great temptation to try, on the chance of luck favoring the marksman."

—Theodore Roosevelt, *Ranch Life and the Hunting-Trail,* The Century Co., 1888

133. Set Your Decoys with Stealth

When hunting pronghorns with a bow, a decoy can make the difference between a fruitless stalk and a successful hunt. The trick is to creep close enough to set one up, and then to set it up without being spotted. Wait until the buck you're hunting is busy chasing a doe, or obscured from view by a clump of sage or other brush. If he sees your decoy rise up out of the grass he may grow suspicious of the unnatural motion and fail to come closer to investigate.

134. Sit over Water

You can avoid strenuous stalks during midday heat if you switch to hunting a water hole. Pronghorns are creatures of the dry, high plains, but they need to drink periodically, and will often show up during the hottest hours to slake their thirst. If you know which water sources they've been using you stand a good chance of ambushing one.

135. Give Your Blind Time

If you plan to hunt from a blind overlooking a water source, make sure the blind has been in place for a few days before you plan to sit in it. Pronghorns will be wary of this new addition to the landscape after it first appears; you want to hunt from it after they grow comfortable enough with its presence to wander within bow range.

136. You Don't Need Long Shots

"The key to getting up on [pronghorns] lies in the seemingly flat land they inhabit, which is actually broken, cut, and intersected by coulees, ravines, gullies, washes, draws, ridges, hills, and divides. A smart antelope hunter can take advantage of this tortured topography to get close—almost always less than 200 yards, and very often less than 100."

—David E. Petzal, "Choosing the Right Rifle for Pronghorn Antelope," www.fieldandstream.com

137. Glass from Your Truck

Most pronghorn antelope have yet to associate vehicles with the hunters who drive them. This makes your truck an idea platform from which to glass for a trophy. Once you've spotted a buck you want to stalk, glass out the route you plan to stalk, then drive your truck far enough away that the animal won't see you getting out.

138. The Pronghorn Antelope's Range

"True Americans, pronghorn are found only on the plains and grasslands of North America. Like bison, seemingly endless numbers once covered the west, stretching from Saskatchewan to just north of Mexico City. And like bison, they nearly became extinct. Populations declined from an estimated 30–60 million in the early 1800s to less than 15,000 by 1915. A moratorium on hunting lasting until the 1940s and a federal tax on firearms and sporting goods funding conservation efforts are credited with stopping the decline. Today there are almost 1 million pronghorn. Five subspecies are recognized: American/common (found in most of range, Canada, and northern Arizona); Mexican/Chihuahuan (found in New Mexico, Texas, formerly southeastern Arizona); Oregon (found in southeastern Oregon); peninsular (100–250 animals, found in Baja, Mexico); and Sonoran (endangered, 500 animals found at Cabeza Prieta National Wildlife Refuge and Sonora, Mexico)."

—Facts About Pronghorns, U.S. Fish & Wildlife Service, www.fws.gov

139. Some Facts of Pronghorn Biology

A male pronghorn weighs, on average, about 120 pounds. Females are slightly smaller, averaging 105 pounds. The animals are not large, standing approximately 3 feet at the shoulder. Both males and females have horns, though the male's are significantly longer, averaging 13 to 15 inches compared to the female's 3- to 5-inch horns. Pronghorns can live up to nine years in the wild.

140. How to Field-Judge a Pronghorn

A trophy antelope's horns will be longer than thirteen inches, which is the distance from the base of an average pronghorn's ear to the tip of its nose. Horns that appear to be twice as long or longer than the animal's ears are likely to break the Boone & Crockett record books, especially if they are curved, crooked, and look wider at their bases than the width of the animal's eye. Look for horns that split into prongs above the tips of an pronghorn's ears. You want an animal whose front prong extends at least 4 inches forward from the main horn.

CHAPTER 9

Wild Sheep and Mountain Goat Hunting

141. North America's Native Wild Sheep

There are two species of wild native sheep in North America, the bighorn sheep and the Dall sheep. There are three subspecies of bighorn: the Rocky Mountain bighorn *(Ovis canadensis canadensis)*, the Sierra Nevada bighorn *(Ovis canadensis sierrae)*, and the desert bighorn *(Ovis canadensis nelsoni)*. There are two subspecies of Dall sheep: the Dall sheep proper and the Stone sheep.

142. Glass in the Morning

Although sheep move most during the morning and evening, it's generally a bad idea trying to find the animals late in the day. Sheep live in high, rough country. Unless you're prepared to spend the night, you don't want to get caught on the side of the mountain in the dark.

143. Watch for Their Rumps

"Bedded sheep will almost always get up and move around a little . . . between noon to around 1 PM. They may feed for a few minutes, or move from one group of beds to another nearby. Or they may only get up, stretch, turn around and lie back down in the same bed. If you are watching the right spot at the right time, you'll see their white rumps and know exactly where they are."

—Bob Hagel, *The Expert's Book of Big Game Hunting in North America*

144. The Colors of the Mountain

Bighorn sheep come in a variety of colors, from light tan to dark brown to a deep blue-gray. These colors vary from region to region (and sometimes within a single region). Because the animals tend to bed in spots that match the colors of their coats, it's a good idea to have a sense of the common shades found in the area you plan to hunt. Look for ground that matches these colors, then look for sheep hidden there.

145. How to Field-Judge a Mountain Goat

Identifying a trophy mountain goat is not easy. The differences between a good billy's and a record-book animal's horns will often be less than an inch. The first step to finding a record is to make sure the animal you've spotted is, in fact, a male. Billies have high, humped shoulders, and shaggier coats than nannies. Once you've found an old male goat, straighten out his horns in your minds eye and compare that length to the length of the animal's head. If the stretched horns reach from the animal's nose to the bottom of its eye, they are less than nine inches long. If they reach from the nose to the base of the ear, they are at least nine inches long and will qualify as a true trophy.

146. Creep across Crests

When stalking sheep and goats, be extremely careful to never silhouette yourself against the skyline. If you must cross the crest of a ridge or a saddle, do so on your hands, knees, and belly, and move as slowly as you can.

147. How to Field-Judge a Trophy Sheep

When glassing for a record-book sheep, always look for a full, curling horn that's bottom extends below the line of the lower jaw. You want heavy, thick horns with broomed tips, which will score higher than unbroomed horns of the same length.

148. Scan for a Silhouette

Sheep easily spot a skylined hunter's silhouette, especially when the hunter is moving. But the reverse is also true. When glassing for sheep, always keep a close eye on the tops of ridges, cliff edges, and the skyline over a saddle. Scanning for silhouettes is the easiest way to spot these animals.

149. Don't Educate the Herd

If you're hunting with friends or as part of a guided group and are lucky enough to kill a sheep, don't immediately rush in to claim your kill after the shot. Stay hidden, watch to see where the animal falls, and wait to retrieve it until the rest of the herd has left the area. Avoid startling them and other hunters in camp will have a much easier time of stalking sheep in the area.

150. Account for the Hump

Don't let an old billy goat's hump throw off your aim. This massive growth of fat and hair covers a ridge of finlike vertebral spines and gives the animal a unique profile when compared with other big game. When preparing to pull the trigger, don't put your crosshairs roughly halfway up a mountain goat's body the way you would on an elk or a deer; the animal's vitals will be located in the lowest third of its body. Hold at the top of that lowest third to ensure a killing shot.

CHAPTER 10

Turkey Hunting

151. Learn to Shoot Turkeys from Both Shoulders

One of the most difficult situations in turkey hunting is having a bird sneak up behind you when you're sitting at the base of a tree. It can be extremely difficult to twist your body around far enough to make an accurate shot, and it's nearly impossible if

the bird is behind your right shoulder if you're a right-handed shooter (and vice versa if you shoot with your left hand forward). It's a good idea to practice shooting your turkey gun from your opposite shoulder before the season starts. If you're comfortable taking shots this way your chances of getting a bead on a turkey without spooking it will improve dramatically.

152. Control the Volume of Your Box Call

If you're working a gobbler with a box call and he hangs up in the distance, you may be calling too strongly. Box calls are notoriously loud; the tom may think the hen you're imitating is closer to him than you want, and will often stop and wait, thinking that she will come to him. One way to get him moving is to reduce the volume of your call. Hold the call upside down, with the handle on the bottom, and slide your thumb up the sides to increase pressure on the call and gradually dampen the vibration. The gobbler will think the hen is moving away from him and may give chase.

153. Five More Reasons Gobblers Are Easy to Miss

Need more reasons to miss a gobbler within 30 yards? Try these: (1) The bird is moving, and you panic slightly, raising your head from the gunstock just a bit; (2) You gun is new, unfamiliar, or one you haven't shot in weeks or months; (3) You're wearing gloves, deadening your touch, and you pull the trigger like it's a rusty nail; (4) Your guide or companion is doing the calling, and he whispers the command "Shoot!" to you. You instantly obey, even though you're not ready; and (5) You try for a head shot. Any of these reasons is enough to make a grown man cry.

154. Use Decoys Late in the Season

The best time to use turkey decoys is after most hens are already sitting on their nests. A decoy is much less effective early in the breeding season when most toms will already be attended by hens.

155. The Best Place to Set Up on a Roosted Gobbler

If you've done your scouting homework, you'll often know where a gobbler has roosted for the night. If you've done your extra credit, you'll know where he goes after he flies down. The best place to set up to call him in the morning will be between these two places, about 100 to 200 yards away from his tree (distance depending on how well leafed out the trees are). Get there well before first light, and sneak in as quietly as you can. Roosted birds are alert to unusual sounds and can pick up movements even in very dark conditions.

156. Don't Let a Hot Gobbler Get Too Close

The next time a gobbling tom comes trotting into your setup, don't wait too long before taking the shot. Most turkey load patterns open up at around 20 to 30 yards; this is the distance at which you have the best chance of putting a pellet into his brain or spine. If you let him get to close your pellets may be packed so tightly together that a slight miscalculation will cause all of them to miss.

157. Locating Roosting Gobblers

When your calling or scouting has located a roosting area (and you've been careful not to spook the birds!), you'll hear them fly up into the trees—big wings flopping, a great deal of noise. Be aware, however, that they don't pick the limb they wish to roost on from the ground, then fly up to it. It's after they are in the trees that they move around to a favored spot to spend the night.

158. When Gobblers Get Lonely

Many turkey hunters miss out on bagging their bird by not being alert to a hunting opportunity that takes place in the middle of the day. Sometimes around eleven o'clock in the morning, hens have left the gobbler to go to their nests. That's when the toms get lonely—and start to gobble, betraying their location. You can get into position, set up, and call in your bird.

159. Rake Leaves to Call in Hung-up Toms

The next time a gobbler hangs up in the distance, responding to your calls but refusing to approach, stop calling and start imitating the sound of a feeding hen by raking a hand through the leaf litter at your feet. If all goes according to plan, the gobbler will grow frustrated, wondering why the hen he can hear scratching for food won't respond to his calls, and will often come closer to investigate.

160. Fake a Flock of Fall Turkeys

Most hunters use turkey decoys to stimulate a gobbler's mating or competitive instincts during the spring season, but decoys also work well for fall turkeys. The trick is to use lots of them to simulate a small flock. If you can figure out where the turkeys you're hunting roost, and where they feed, set up your fake flock between them and use a couple of different calls to imitate the sound of a few feeding hens.

161. Circle Gobbling Birds Hung up behind Obstacles

Gobbling turkeys hang up for lots of reasons, but one of the most common is that there's an obstacle between him and you. Streams, fences, and ravines will often keep a turkey from following up on the promise of a ready hen. In many cases you'll have the best luck killing your bird by crossing these barriers yourself. Using a crow call to keep him gobbling, circle around him until you're 180-degrees away from where you were set up before. He'll be more likely to return along a path he's already used than he will to work through less familiar territory, and you'll know there won't be any other obstacles on this trail that might obstruct his progress.

162. Faking Out a Gobbler: A Desperation Tactic

When a gobbler plays hard to get, and nothing else has worked try walking straight away from him, calling occasionally as you go. If he thinks his potential paramour is leaving him, he just might come running.

163. Cover Ground to Find Mid-Day Gobblers

Turkeys gobble more in the early morning than they do during the middle of the day. This makes them easier to find, but it does not mean they are easier to hunt. Most toms will gobble in the morning even if they're with hens, which means you stand a good chance of spending all morning talking with a bird that has no reason to come to your calls. If you find yourself working a bird that refuses to come to you, don't give up hope. Instead, go looking for a more accommodating tom. It is true that turkeys gobble less frequently when the sun is high, but the flip side of this behavior is that if you find one that does gobble, he is much less likely to be with a hen and will be far more willing to come in to your calls. Hike through your property and call every 100 yards or so until you get a response.

164. Don't Get Mistaken for a Turkey

Never wear any clothing or carry any accessories that contain the colors red, white, or blue. You should also keep your hands and head camouflaged when calling, and wear dark-colored socks and pants long enough to keep bare skin fully covered. These colors are found on the heads of wild turkeys, and you do not want to be mistaken for a gobbler by another hunter.

165. Make a Gobbler Jealous

You can use a decoy to simulate a breeding hen by pushing a hen decoy's stake deeply enough into the soil so that the decoy's belly touches the ground. Hens take this position when they're ready to mate. Put a jake decoy behind her (a jake is an

immature male turkey), as if he's about to breed her, and the tom you're hunting may become so upset that he approaches your setup with much less caution.

166. Bust a Roosted Flock in the Fall

The most common tactic used by fall turkey hunters is to find and then scatter a flock of the birds and then sit down to call them back in. Turkeys will naturally want to regroup, and if you call well enough to imitate a lost bird, they will use you as a homing beacon. One good way to find a flock to bust is

to identify where the birds roost. Scout the woods for large hardwood trees with lots of fresh droppings at their bases, and head out the evening before you plan to hunt to listen for the sounds the birds make as they fly up for the night. Creep into the woods before sunrise the next day, and then rush the flock as soon as it flies down.

167. Coping with "Shut-Mouth" Gobblers

If pressure has forced spring gobblers into silence, try patterning a long beard like you would a deer. He'll have favorites route he takes to favored strutting areas and feeding spots. So glass open areas until you find where the birds are using, then set up an ambush.

168. Don't Waste Time on Henned-Up Birds When You Can Hunt Somewhere Else

If you've got lots of land to hunt, don't waste time trying to bring in turkeys that aren't that interested in your calling. When a bird gobbles once in response to your calls but won't move any closer after 15 to 20 minutes, it's likely he's still with hens. Make a mental note of your location, then move on to search for another, lonelier bird who will respond with more enthusiasm. Later, however, if you still haven't filled your tag, return to the spot you were calling in when you first heard him

gobble and try calling again. His hens may now be on their nests, and he'll be wondering what happened to the one that wouldn't come see him earlier in the morning.

169. Why Gobblers Are Easy to Miss

How do hunters miss a big target like a wild turkey standing within 30 yards? My personal pet theory (and I've done it myself!) is that the shooter is so enthralled by the scene before him that he raises his head from the gunstock just slightly. Do that, and you'll miss every time.

170. When Roosting Gobblers Fly Down

When you hear hens fly down from the roost, while a gobbler lingers on his limb, still calling occasionally, your nerves will be as tight as they can get. But don't start thinking your bird is as good as in the oven. Next, a scenario can take place that virtually dooms your hunt. The hens may start walking away in a direction away from your setup. The gobbler flies down and joins them, oblivious to your calls.

CHAPTER 11

Duck Hunting

171. Wind and Your Decoy Setups

The truth is that you can spread your duck decoys just about any way you wish, as long as you leave an open area for the birds to land into the wind. No matter which way they come from, or how much they circle, their final move down will be into the wind. No wind at all? It becomes a guessing game.

172. Guide's Advice I Don't Want to Hear

In the duck blind, you'll often hear your guide urge you to, "Stay down. Keep your head down. Don't watch the birds! I'll do the watching." Well, if you're not watching the birds, you're losing part of the joys of the hunt. Your blind should be good enough for you to peer through the stalks or brush just as the

guide is doing. When the ducks are passing right overhead, neither one of you should be looking skyward. You'll spook the birds for sure.

173. Pothole Sneak Attack

If you've scouted out a promising pothole or small pond and you're planning to jump-shoot the ducks that are resting there,

try to sneak up on them with the wind at your back. When the ducks jump into the wind (which they most certainly will do), you might get a shot before they re-orient themselves and fly the other way.

174. Local Birds: Use Small Decoy Spreads for Small Bunches

Make a distinction between the resident ducks you hunt in early season and the large flocks that migrate in later on. You'll spot resident birds in pairs and small flocks, so decoy them accordingly and don't burn out any one place by hunting it too often. Save the big spreads for when the birds from up north show up.

175. Mix 'Em up If You Want To

So you're thinking about adding some bluebills or canvasbacks (diving ducks) to your decoy setup of mallards, pintails, and gadwalls (puddle ducks) to give your spread more visibility. Go right ahead. It won't hurt your chances a bit.

176. Jump-Shooting Joys

Jump-shooting ducks from a canoe or john-boat is a great way to hunt some creeks and small rivers. The best way is with a

partner, one hunter with the gun at the ready, the other on the paddling. Stay quiet, anticipate the sharp bends where you may surprise a few mallards, blacks, or other puddle ducks. Listen carefully as you go. You just might hear the birds before you get to them.

177. Too Hidden for a Good Shot

When you're hunkered down in a blind so that you can't see the ducks you're working, when it comes time for someone to exclaim, "Take 'em!" you come up with your gun and have to find the birds before you get down to pointing and swinging the barrel. It won't be an easy shot.

178. Gloves for Setting out Decoys

Gloves that stretch almost to your elbows and keep your hands dry are a must for setting out decoys. Shuck 'em off and wear your regular gloves when you get into the blind. See the "Midwest PVC Decoy Glove" at Mack's Prairie Wings, www.mackspw.com. Check other favorite waterfowl gear vendors for other options.

179. Pond Shooting at Sunset: The Way It Used to Be

Waiting for ducks at sunset beside ponds where the ducks would be coming to roost was once a mainstay of hunting

tactics. Local wood ducks, mallards, and black ducks, puddle ducks of all sorts that had migrated into a particular area—they all come hurtling into the ponds after sunset. Sometimes the shooting was so late, the birds had to be outlined against the western sky. Today, shooters who try this are easy marks for wardens waiting nearby to hear the sounds of gunshots after legal shooting hours. If you want to just watch the show (and you should!) leave your guns in the truck.

180. It's All about Visibility, Visibility, Visibility

Unless you're gunning a tiny creek-bottom or river location, surrounded by high trees, most of your duck-hunting locations will be in open areas where you hope passing birds can see your decoys and come on in. Anything you can do to increase the visibility of your spread will make a difference. Black decoys show up better from a distance. Magnum-size adds visibility. Canada geese decoys add visibility, whether you're hunting geese or not. Movement devices (the ones that are legal where you hunt) are critical if there's no wind blowing: spinners, battery-driven shakers, pull-cord movers—whatever you've got.

181. The "Hole" Is the Thing

No matter what shape of decoy spread you decide is right for your hunting location and conditions, it must contain a hole or two for the birds to land. If the water in front of the blind is solid with decoys, the birds will land on the outside of the spread, at long range or even out of range.

182. The Outer Gun: The Key Position

The Outside shooter on the upwind side of permanent duck blinds or lay-out blind setups is in the key position and can absolutely ruin the shooting for everybody with him. It's happened to me more times than I can remember. The ducks, or geese, are coming into the spread against the wind, from his side. If he starts shooting too early, around the corner, the guns in the center and other side will get no shots, or shots at widely flaring birds only. Sometimes, to top off this little drama, the outside offender will turn to the other guys and say, "Why didn't you guys shoot?" Advice: Put an experienced shooter in that outside position, a shooter with the judgment and nerve to wait until the birds are into the spread enough so everybody can shoot.

183. Where'd the Mallards Go?

When you're on a marsh in the early morning where you reasonably expect a flight of mallards, don't be surprised if they don't show up until later in the morning. Your local birds, or even visitors from the north, may be feeding in the fields.

184. Black Ducks—Red Letter Day

My calling aspirations reached a sort of pinnacle years later. I was hunkered on an icy creek on the marshes of the Chesapeake Bay, near the famous Susquehanna Flats. A pair of black ducks flew down the creek, very high and in a big hurry, headed somewhere with express tickets. They clearly were not interested in my modest decoy spread, but when I hit them with my old Herter's call and the Highball, they turned like I had 'em wired. Interested then, they circled warily while I scrunched down. Now I started rattling off my Feeding Chuckle, and a few moments later they were cupped and committed. I could finally say that I knew how to call ducks.

185. Where the Birds Want to Be

Pushing into a cove in the marsh or along a big river or lake, in the first pre-dawn light, you flush a big bunch of ducks or geese. Away they go, gabbling and honking. Never mind trying to follow them or heading for another spot. Set up right there. It's the place the birds want to be.

186. "Take 'Em!"

Few moments afield are as thrilling as those when a big flock of ducks sweeps into your decoys. You'll shoot a lot better when you are aware whether your birds are diving ducks—like bluebills and canvasbacks—or puddle ducks—like mallards and pintails. Diving ducks will bore straight past when the shooting starts, while puddle ducks will bounce skyward as though launched from a trampoline.

187. Tall-Timber Trick

When gunning the hole in the tall timber with a few decoys out, give the water around your tree a good kick when birds are passing or circling to imitate splashing and feeding activity.

188. Using the Wind with Your Decoy Spread

Ducks often want to land outside a spread of decoys—even when the setup has left an inviting hole. That's why you want to set your decoys upwind—not directly in front of the blind—so that you'll still have a good shot at the birds coming in against the wind and trying to land on the outside of the decoy spread.

189. Don't Be a "Skybuster"

A "skybuster" is the most hated person on any marsh or field where there's duck or goose hunting. The Skybuster blazes away at birds that are clearly out of range, thereby frightening the birds away from the area and ruining chances others might have had on the incoming birds.

190. Beating the Crowds in Public Hunting

Ducks quickly wise up to blinds on public hunting areas. You score more ducks if you seek out remote corners that see much less pressure. Use just a half dozen or so decoys and call only enough to get passing birds' interest.

CHAPTER 12

Goose Hunting

191. The Most Effective Way to Set Out Goose Decoys

Veteran Maryland call-maker Sean Mann guides early season duck and goose hunting in Alberta and is one of the most successful and experienced in the business. He told DU's Wade

Bourne, in a tip for the DU Web site: "To finish more geese when hunting over a field spread, set decoys 10 feet apart (three long steps), and face them in random directions. This set provides a natural, relaxed look, and it also offers incoming birds plenty of landing room inside the spread. By setting my decoys so far apart, I use half the number I used to. I can set up and tear down faster, and most of all, the geese work better. Our hunts are much more productive than when I set decoys closer together. Less really can be more."

192. How to Change Your Luck with Snow Geese

In the October '08 *Field & Stream,* author Dave Hurteau, in an interview with veteran guide Tracy Northup, Up North Outdoors, www.huntupnorth.com, presents a deadly method for changing your luck with those tough, high-flying flocks of snow geese. In a tip called, "Play the Wind," Northup says. "Snow geese typically fly high and circle straight down, making

it difficult to shoot them anywhere but right over a good spread. But a 30–40-mph wind keeps them flying nice and low." Northup recommends scouting out a location of snows where there are ditches or hedgerows a hundred yards or so from the fields where you can sneak into position to pick off the low-flying snows as they pass—without spooking the main flock.

193. Birds in Flight: Looks Are Deceiving

Because they are big, Canada Geese appear to be slow in flight, compared to ducks. And because of their long tails, pheasants appear to be slower than they really are. Swing your gun properly, lead the bird, and keep swinging as you pull the trigger. Or you'll be shaking your head, wondering how you missed.

194. Snow Geese: Playing the Numbers Game

Those large flocks of snow geese weaving across the horizon, clamoring constantly, are hard to pull into normal decoy spreads of just two- or three-dozen birds. The flying geese can see great distances, and they are looking for big groups of feeding birds. Savvy hunters have learned to cope with this by putting out decoys by the hundreds, if necessary, and to do this they'll use all the silhouettes they can haul to the site, plus whatever "rag-type" decoys they can fashion themselves from things like baby diapers and white garbage bags attached to a stake.

195. Layout Blinds Take Getting Used To

When using a layout blind, before the birds start flying take some time to try practicing the move it takes to rise into a shooting position. It takes some getting used to. If you don't practice it, you may not be in a good position with your face well down on the gun during the first critical seconds when it's time to, take 'em!

196. When the Canadas Sleep Late

In below-zero weather, sleep in an extra hour or two. When it's that cold Canadas will stay roosted and fly out to feed only after the sun has come up and warmed things up a bit. It might be 10 AM before they leave the roost. The only thing you'll get by showing up at dawn is cold.

197. Keep Those Silhouettes Visible

When using silhouette decoys for geese, take care to position them so many of them appear broadside at every angle. When edge-on to the viewpoint of the flying birds, they become invisible.

198. Layout Blinds: You're Part of the Action

You're lying in a field, totally hidden right among the decoys. No brushy blind, no boat, no pit blind, no elaborate box blind, no blind on stilts. Instead, you're tucked comfortably into a well-camouflaged layout blind, made further invisible by attaching brush to the blind's convenient straps and holders. You're wearing camo yourself, including a hat and mask. Even your gun is camouflaged. Unlike hunting from a brush blind where you have to keep your face down—and thereby miss part of the spectacle of flying birds on the way in—you're seeing the whole show, from the time birds appear in the distance, until they coming right into your face. There's nothing like it!

199. Hiding Your Boat in Plain Sight

The john-boat or canoe you can put into the water and go wherever the ducks and geese are flying has gotten a lot easier to hide with the introduction of today's synthetic camo material. The material, imitating different shades and textures of marsh grass, comes in manageable mats you can attach to your boat, then roll up and put away after your hunt. Cabela's, www.cabelas.com, has a bunch of different patterns, including the excellent Avery, and there's a popular one called Fast-Grass that's available at the Knutson's waterfowling store and site, www.knutsondecoys.com.

200. Don't Let Those Incoming Geese Fool You

"The approach of wild geese to a blind is one of the neatest optical illusions in nature. The geese just keep on coming. You think they are one hundred yards away, and they are two hundred. You think they are fifty yards away, and they are one hundred."

—Gordon MacQuarrie, "Geese! Get Down!," *Field & Stream,* 1941, reprinted in *The Field & Stream Reader,* Doubleday, 1946

CHAPTER 13

Grouse and Woodcock Hunting

201. Good Hearing Can Pay Off Big

When the leaves in the woods are dry and crinkly, say on a perfect Indian Summer day, you can actually hear the few steps ruffed grouse take to launch into flight. The sound is a sort of dry, "tick, tick." Once you've heard it a couple of times, followed by a flushing bird, you'll know what to listen for.

202. Grouse Hunting Teamwork

It's fun to hunt grouse with a buddy, but you must know each other's location at all times, and even then you may not be able to take a shot. (That's the very reason most grouse hunters shoot better when they're hunting alone.) In keeping track of one another, use a simple call-out, like, "Ho!" or "Over Here!" instead of constantly shouting sentences like, "I'm over here, Bob, on your right." The more grouse hear of such talk, the more likely they are to flush wild.

203. Second Shots on Early Season Grouse Coveys

When you flush a couple of early season grouse, and fire only one shot, don't break your gun to reload right away. You may be into an entire group of birds hatched that year, and one of the birds that's been sitting tight will jump late—just when you break open your gun. On the other hand, if you've fired both shells, try to reload as quickly as possible.

204. Keep Track of Where You Shot From

Woodcocks are small birds and their feathers make for excellent camouflage on the forest floor. This can make finding one you've shot hard to retrieve, especially if you're hunting without a dog. After you knock one down, hang your hat on a branch or drop a spent shell on the ground where you were standing when you pulled the trigger. If you get confused about where you thought the bird landed you'll be able to return to the exact place you shot from to restart your search.

205. Cock Bird or a Hen? How to Tell

The black band on the tail of all ruffed grouse tells you whether you've bagged a male or female. The cock bird always has a continuous band, while the hen's is broken. As in all things in nature, there are exceptions sometimes, mostly among young birds.

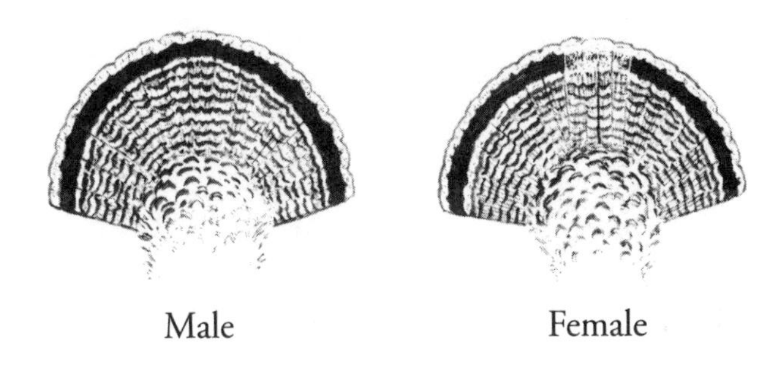

Male Female

206. Noise Flushes More Grouse

Yes, grouse can be a tight-holding bird, but when you're approaching their location with a lot of chatter and constant commands to your dog, you're almost guaranteeing you'll get a wild flush, out ahead of the point.

207. Flushing Dogs as Grouse Dogs

It makes a lot of sense to use flushing/retrieving dogs like Labs, Springers, and Goldens as grouse and woodcock dogs.

(Pheasants too, by the way.) In addition to flushing the birds, they retrieve and make great family dogs. When trained properly to hunt close to the gun, these dogs can do a good job for you in grouse and woodcock covers. When not properly trained, running wide distances and out of control, they are worse than useless. You'd be better off walking up your birds alone.

208. The Perfect Grouse and Woodcock Gun

When it comes to grouse guns, arguments may rage over the bore—12 or 20 gauge—but you'll find general agreement over these details: lightweight, short barrel, fast swinging, and with a stock that fits so perfectly that it instantly becomes part of you when your face touches the stock.

209. Hitting More Grouse: The Big Secret

Here it comes, the grouse-hunting technique that will put more birds in your coat than any other: When you hear the flush, don't stand there looking for the bird, then raise your gun. Your gun should be coming to

your shoulder as you look toward the direction of the flush. At the first glimpse of the bird, the barrel should be coming onto what you're seeing, and you fire instantly. There's no tracking, no aiming. It's a "throw" shot, as I prefer to call it, instead of the oft-heard "snap" shot. Of course, this method is assuming a hunting buddy is behind you, out of harm's way.

210. The Dead "Giveaway" on Woodcock

"Going into strange woodcock terrain 'cold' can be disappointing. Two coverts may look alike, yet only one many attract

'cock. Whitewash is the best clue, next to seeing actual birds. The white splashing disintegrate rapidly and when you see them you can almost count on woodcock being nearby."

—George Bird Evans, *The Upland Shooting Life*,
Knopf, 1971

CHAPTER 14

Pheasant Hunting

211. When Ringnecks Sit Tight

Despite their reputation for being track stars, running ahead of the dogs and hunters, pheasants are capable of making

themselves invisible and sitting tight when they feel pressured enough. They can hide in the smallest clump of grass, letting you walk right past them.

212. Don't Let That Tail Fool You

Compared to gamebirds like quail and ruffed grouse, the take-off of a pheasant, while exciting, is rather slow. However, in its initial, vaulting leap, the rooster pheasant's long tail and gaudy colors make the bird seem even larger than it really is, and the shooter fails to take a lead, but merely pokes the barrel at the body of the bird.

213. How "Cackles" Betray Cockbirds

When a pheasant "cackles" as it flushes, it's a cockbird. Every time. Hens do not cackle. This doesn't mean that cockbirds cackle every time they flush. They don't. Sometimes they fly away in silence. But when you hear a cackling bird, even if it's in the sun and you can't see its colors, you know it's a cockbird.

214. Go Late for Western Ringnecks

While the typical western ringneck hunt involves following short tails though long, golden grass in shirt-sleeve weather, some of the best pheasant hunting on prime habitats in the Dakotas, Nebraska, and Montana occurs after Thanksgiving. There is less

pressure then, and the winter weather tends to push birds into flocks. Gaining access to great hunting spots is often easier then, with big game seasons ended. So consider a late season pheasant hunt in the West.

215. The Key Maneuver

When you work pheasant cover, always work toward a distinct end point, be it an irrigation ditch, road, creek, or open field. The birds will eventually figure they can't outrun you. As you and your dog approach that end point, the birds will flush.

216. You're Walking Past the Birds

Pheasants tend to sit tighter in wet weather, so work cover more thoroughly than you would on a bluebird day.

217. Coming up Empty!

Always reload quickly after shooting a flushing rooster; he may have compatriots with him. While you're patting yourself on the back for a great shot, other birds may flush as you stand there with an empty shotgun.

218. They Need to Take a Drink

Like four-legged critters, pheasants need a water source to thrive. In dry months in the fall, work cover near watering holes late in the afternoon to find birds.

219. Pheasants in the Tracking Snow

Got snow? Then go track up a pheasant. You don't need a dog, and you'll quickly learn the

birds' favorite hiding spots and get a good feel of how many birds are in the area.

220. After the Season Opens . . .

Hunting pheasants on opening day and then a week later will seem like the difference between night and day. The pheasant's "disappearing act" after opening day is one of the most remarkable in all upland bird hunting.

CHAPTER 15

Quail Hunting

221. Shooting the Covey Rise

A good covey rise—say twelve to fifteen birds—is one of the most exciting events in all wing-shooting. Alas, it's also the time when many shooters miss on their first shot, then hastily throw their second shot into thin air. From Day One, quail hunters are urged, "Pick out one bird and shoot it." But they

have a hard time doing it. The sight of all those birds, particularly wild birds, hurtling toward the trees—or even through the trees—keeps their face from getting down on the stock, which will result in a miss every time. Some hunters do well on coveys by telling themselves that they're going to shoot the first bird that flies—just as though they were shooting singles. In my case, my scores on covey rises improved when I started really hunkering down on the gun, swinging toward one bird, and telling myself, "I'm going to kill that bird." That's the kind of focus shooting covey rises requires, at least in my view."

222. Leave That Safety on until the Shot!

In my formative gun-handling years, I learned to leave the safety on until the gun is moving toward my shoulder to make a shot. Many quail hunters take their safeties off when walking in to a point to flush the birds. The practice is dangerous. The birds may have moved, the dog will have to relocate, and you might have a lot more walking before the birds take flight (if indeed they ever do take flight). Walking around through briars and tangles with a loaded gun with the safety off is a prescription for disaster. Train yourself to leave the safety on until a bird is in the air and the gun is moving toward your shoulder.

223. Marking down the Singles

After a covey rise, many hunters make the mistake of diverting their attention to downed birds too quickly, instead of carefully watching the escape routes of the covey's survivors. Even after these escaping birds are seen to cup their wings and sail in a certain direction, they bear careful watching, for they can sail a long way and change direction quickly.

224. Cold Front Moving in—Great Hunting!

There's nothing quite like being in the field in an afternoon when low clouds are scudding about, it's starting to spit just a bit of snow or icy rain, and the temperature has been dropping sharply. Quail will be feeding like there's no tomorrow, leaving strong trails of scent your dogs can easily find. You can bag your limit on a day like this.

225. Make Mine a Side-by-Side

All right, call me "old-fashioned" if you wish. But to me, a side-by-side 20-gauge double is the gun of choice for bobwhite quail. Barrels 26 inches, bored modified and improved cylinder. You can tramp a long time with a light double, enjoying its sweet feel of balance and sleekness, and when the gun comes to your shoulder, the broad sighting plane seems to flow onto the target. I like double triggers, and a straight stock, but again, I'm old-fashioned. For many hunters today, the over-under seems to be the favorite, especially when it's the same gun used for sporting clays. Makes all the sense in the world. But it's not for me in the quail woods.

226. Leave Some for "Seed"

Shooting a covey of wild bobwhites down to two or three birds doesn't make any sense. From a covey of say twelve birds, set your personal take as five or six. No more. Now leave that covey alone for the rest of the season. There's always next year.

227. Keep Your Head down on the Stock

Hunters sometimes wonder why they missed a seemingly easy shot—a covey of quail bursting into flight, a flock of mallards right over the decoys, even a wild turkey strutting into plain view. Often the reason is simply because your were so excited and enthralled by what you are seeing, that you lift your head slightly from the gunstock. When you do, it's all over! You're going to miss the shot.

228. Take It Easy, Get More Shots

With a good bird dog willing to "hunt close" under today's tough conditions, quail hunting is not the place to be in a hurry. Instead, just mosey along and take your time, working every nook and cranny along the edges of the fields thoroughly. You'll find lots more coveys than the hunter in a hurry.

229. When Birds Are Running, Keep up with Your Dog

When your dog is pointing for a few seconds, then moving ahead, then moving again and relocating as you come up, you've obviously got some running birds ahead. Try to keep up with the dog as he moves along. Chances are high that this covey is going to flush wild, well ahead.

230. They're Closer Than You Think

"Most quail are killed within sixty feet of the gun. Before you say I am wrong, measure the next ten you kill. The bobwhite fades away so fast on the flush that many men won't shoot at a bird thirty to thirty-five yards away, believing that he is beyond good killing range."

—Ray P. Holland, *Scattergunning*, Knopf, 1951

CHAPTER 16

Squirrel Hunting

231. Staying Put on Your Stand

When you've selected a good spot to sit and wait for squirrels to show themselves, don't be in a hurry to walk over and pick up the first two or three you down—with shotgun or rifle. Mark them carefully and keep sitting tight and watch for another target to show.

232. The "Trunk-Hugger" Squirrel

When a squirrel hugs the trunk, high in the tree and not moving, it usually is facing up the tree. By hugging the trunk yourself, you can outlast the squirrel into thinking the coast is clear. It will make a move, giving you a shot.

233. A Squirrel Hunt Can Make Your Day Great

Many hunters get so caught up in the pursuit of deer and "glamour" upland birds like grouse, quail, and pheasant that they forget the simple pleasures of a great day out squirrel hunting. Take a golden autumn day, a small pack with sandwiches and a thermos, a scope-sighted .22 rifle, and local knowledge of an area and you can walk for miles—that is, walk when you wish to. A lot of your day will be spent sitting quietly at the basses of trees, watching the canopy overhead. One caveat: You can't do this hunt when and where firearm deer hunting is in progress.

234. Playing "Hide-and-Seek" with Squirrels

When a squirrel is on the opposite side of a tree, and keeps going around and around as you circle, trying to get a shot, try throwing something noisy over to the squirrel's side. A heavy fallen stick or something. You can often move him to your side this way.

235. Those Wonderful Squirrel Dogs

They'll never have the glamour and appeal of labs and pointers and setters, but good squirrel dogs are worth their weight in gold. What kind are they? All kinds! Feists, curs, whatever. A good nose and desire to hunt are the credentials, and the best way to take advantage of them is to have your squirrel dog

puppy hunt with an accomplished squirrel dog. The really good squirrel dogs hunt close to the gun and use their nose, eyes, and ears to find squirrels. Easing slowly through the squirrel woods with one of these dogs is a wonderful way to go hunting. In many areas, you'll have a bonus: You'll flush coveys of quail, and send rabbits bouncing away.

236. Cutting-Edge Squirrel Loads

In a comprehensive article called "Cutting-Edge Squirrel Loads" on the *Game & Fish* magazine Web site, www.gameandfishmag.com, writer Mike Bleech gives today's squirrel hunters the latest details on shotgun and rifle loads that do the best job in bringing home a limit of bushytails. Bleech examines the important differences in magnum versus standard shot loads, with emphasis on the all-important velocity considerations. He brings the .22 hunter right up to date with test-firing comparing the venerable .22 Long Rifle against the scorching hot newcomer the .17 Hornady Magnum Rimfire and the newer, but slower, Hornady .17M2. The .17M2 gets Bleech's nod as the best way to go because, as he says, "The light crack of the .17M2 is barely noticed by the squirrels."

237. Mast Crop Low, yet Hunting Great

When the crop of acorns on the white and red oaks is low, look for squirrels to be concentrated in areas where some trees have bucked the trend. Whatever good spots for acorns are available, the squirrels will find them—particularly the white oak acorns. White-tailed deer do the same.

238. The Pecan Tree Bonanza

The shady, fruit-bearing groves of pecan trees planted throughout the southeast and on into Texas are squirrel magnets. Forested edges of the groves will hold good populations of squirrels. With the landowners' permissions, you'll be set for good hunting.

239. Midwinter Fox Squirrels

When there's a crust of snow on the ground and the temperatures have dipped into the 20s, don't expect fox squirrels to be on the prowl in early morning. You'll find the best hunting doesn't get started until around ten o'clock. Although like gray squirrels, fox squirrels like acorns and other nuts, in midwinter they will always head for corn if it's nearby. Fox squirrels prefer belts of trees near croplands instead of dense forests, more so than grays.

240. Try More Aggressive Squirrel Tactics

Successful squirrel hunters today have come as many calls and calling techniques as duck hunters. Consider these two examples: On the Hunter Specialties Web site, www.hunterspec.com, pro Alex Rutledge shows how to use the H.S. Squirrel Call to do the "Barking," "Chattering," and the "Young Squirrel Distress Call." All are effective, but "Barking" is one known to set off a chorus of squirrel answering calls and tip off their locations in woods you're hunting for the first time. Outdoor writer John E. Phillips, in his "John's Journal," on his Night Hawk Publications site, www.nighthawkpublications.com, also likes "Barking," along with some other calls he describes in his article, "How to Hunt Squirrels Aggressively."

CHAPTER 17

Rabbit Hunting

241. The Hunter's "Rabbit's Foot" Luck

Rabbits are the Number One game for hunters everywhere—and with good reason. They breed like crazy, which is great since few of them survive the predators they face for even one year. There are still plenty to go around for hunters, who prize delicious rabbit on their tables and like the way rabbits can be hunted with a variety of methods and a minimum of expensive gear.

242. Watching for the Rabbit You've Jumped

When your dog is running a rabbit, don't keep your eyes locked on the path the dog is taking. Keep looking in other directions, and you may spot rabbits that are trying to slip past all the action, or others that are just sitting tight waiting for you to go past.

243. Top Tips for Late Season Rabbits

Late season is a great time to hunt rabbits because deer hunters have ceased activities. Hunting can be tough, though. According to writer Ed Harp on the Indiana state site of *Game & Fish* magazine, www.indianagameandfish.com, the most important four considerations in finding late season rabbits are to find the clover, find blackberry and raspberry bushes, find the pine sapling stands where rabbits have chewed the bark in a circle, and find deer hunter food plots. Harp has six more top tips to help you get your limit in the article, "Ten Tips for Taking Winter Rabbits."

244. Use a Stick to Beat the Brush

When hunting rabbits without a dog, use a brush stick, like a wading staff, to beat on the edges of thick cover where they may be hiding.

245. Cold and Windy Mornings

On a windy morning, after a very cold night, look for rabbits to be on the sunny and lee sides of ridges, forests, and brush rows.

246. Hunting the "Slabfoot" Rabbits

He's not called the "Varying Hare" for nothing, possessing two coats of fur to wear as needed. With the fall sun starts riding lower and lower in the sky, the days becoming shorter and shorter, the Snowshoe rabbit starts putting on its white coat whether needed or not by snowfall. Even with nary a flake on the ground, the big hares begin to change color—a dangerous situation for them since they stand out in the forest so starkly. In Alaska, where I spent two teenage winters, Snowshoe rabbit hunting became a big part of my life. I loved hunting them and eating them.

247. Snowshoes in Winter: The Going Gets Tough

The hunting in the hills not far from Fairbanks, where we lived, was easy until the snows came, then became more difficult with each passing day. The Snowshoe is mostly a nocturnal animal. During the day the rabbits hole up under the endless spruces and don't move until after dark. Kicking them out is tough work without a dog. When we were lucky enough to get one bounding away through the snow, they were remarkably fast and hard to hit in their great leaps over the snow. Old "Slab-foot." I loved them.

248. The Snowshoes' Survival Plan

When winter grips the great North woods, the icy winds moaning through bare limbs without a scrap of vegetation, the snow piling on the endless spruce forests, the Snowshoe rabbit makes out just fine. Gone are the succulent plants of spring and summer, but the "Varying Hares" do just fine on a diet of willow, poplar, and other saplings of tender green bark. The Snowshoe has four big front teeth perfect for gnawing a bellyful of bark every night. Days are spent in cozy holes back under the spruces. No matter how cold, they make out just fine.

249. Tactic for Snowshoes: Leave the Feeding Grounds Behind

The area where you find the great crisscrossing webs of Snowshoe tracks may not be the best place to make your hunt. They were there last night feeding; now they're dead certain to be in the thickest cover of the nearest swamps. That's where you want to make your hunt, moving slowly past the beaver dams, humps of brush, fallen trees, and limbs—the places where Snowshoes spend their days, not their nights.

250. Your Best Rabbit "Scouts"

The best rabbit scout you can find will be the farmer who owns the land you hunt on. Next will be the deer hunters who've been working the area. Many of them aren't interested in rabbit hunting, but they will have seen the spots where rabbits thrive.